THINGS TO DO IN AMSTERDAM: MUSEUMS

MARKO KASSENAAR

LIESBETH HEENK

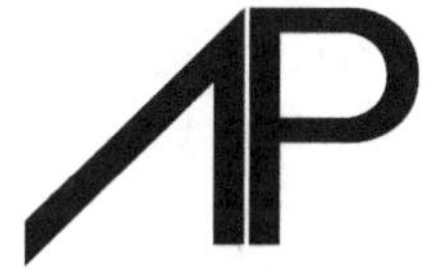

CONTENTS

RIJKSMUSEUM

ANNE FRANK HOUSE

VAN GOGH MUSEUM

HERMITAGE AMSTERDAM

ISBN 13: 9789492371775 (ebook)

ISBN 13: 9789492371768 (paperback)

The publisher can be reached at info@amsterdampublishers.com

RIJKSMUSEUM

HIGHLIGHTS OF THE COLLECTION

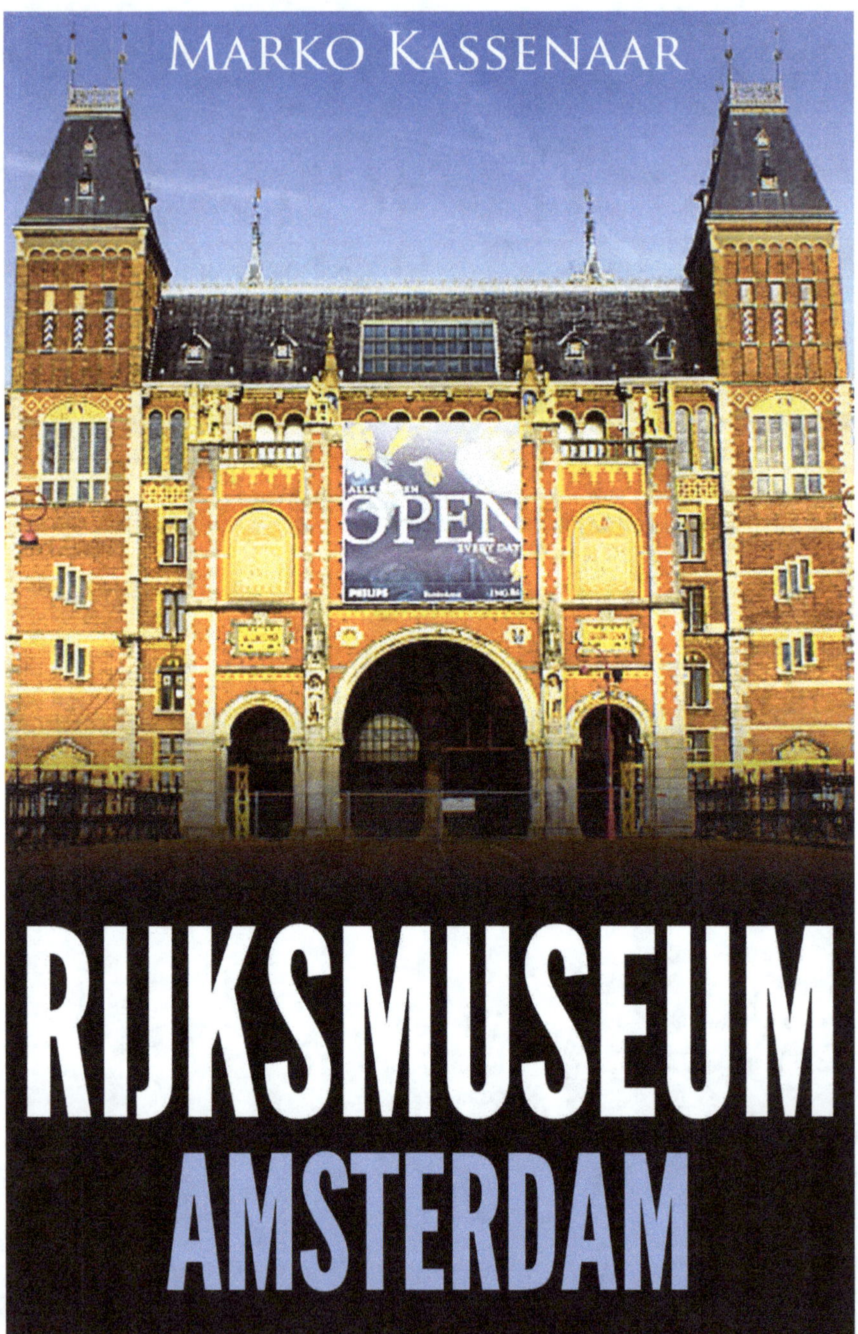

MARKO KASSENAAR
OPEN
RIJKSMUSEUM
AMSTERDAM

'The country's divine sons, united in this Pantheon'
(*Excerpt from a poem celebrating the opening of the Rijksmuseum - 1885*)

'A feel for beauty, a sense of time'
(*Motto of the Rijksmuseum - 2013*)

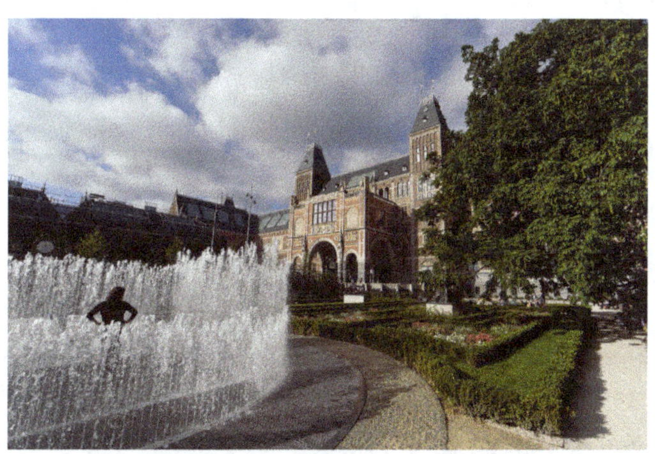

Rijksmuseum Amsterdam, photo by Evgeny Prokofyev

INTRODUCTION

The Rijksmuseum (Dutch for 'National Museum') houses the biggest and most important art collection of the Netherlands. The cathedral-like building contains the works of the 17th-century Dutch Masters such as Rembrandt, Vermeer and Hals. The museum also boasts a world famous collection of Asian art, Dutch doll's houses and Meissen porcelain. In total, the Rijksmuseum guards over 1,1 million objects. The most famous and prestigious work of the Rijksmuseum collection is *The Night Watch* by Rembrandt van Rijn.

In the Rijksmuseum you literally walk through history. Every section of the museum is dedicated to a specific century. In each room, works of various art disciplines are exhibited together. This combination of paintings and objects lets you experience the atmosphere of different periods in time.

You can, for example, visit a 17th-century painting gallery or an 18th-century 'style room' decorated with tapestries and ornamental stucco. Medieval and Renaissance art is on display in the basement vaults.

The Rijksmuseum building is a work of art in itself. Architect Pierre Cuypers (1827 - 1921) designed it as a temple where the gods of Dutch art would reside. The result looks like a mixture of a cathedral and a gigantic Amsterdam canal house.

During recent renovations, a spacious atrium was created in the inner courtyards of the building. In the atrium you can buy your tickets, visit the museum shop or relax in the cafeteria.

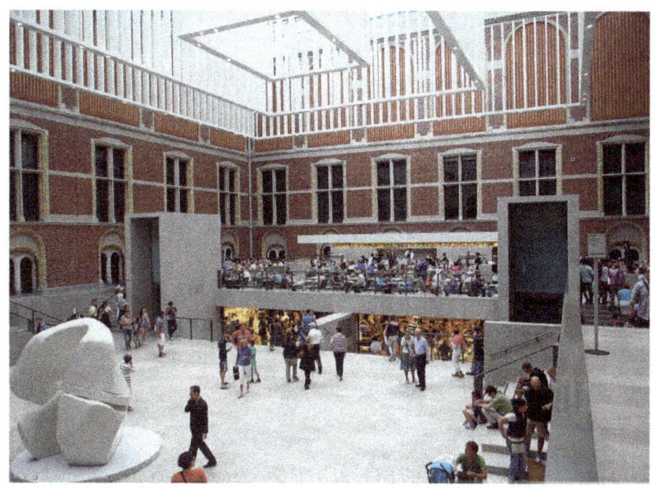

The Atrium of the Rijksmuseum, Copyright Wikimedia

TIP: RIJKS® is the Rijksmuseum's restaurant in the Philips Wing. This lively brasserie has been awarded a Michelin star and serves great food. The Rijksmuseum itself has a café (with lunch menu) and three espresso bars.

GALLERY OF HONOR AND 17TH-CENTURY ART

The main collection of the Rijksmuseum consists of paintings by the Dutch Masters of the 17th century such as Rembrandt, Vermeer and Hals. This period in history is known, both economically and artistically, as the Dutch Golden Age. The Netherlands were a world power with rulers spending lots of money on art and science. Besides paintings, there is a collection of silverware, furniture, earthenware and glass.

The 17th-century collection is exhibited in the Front Hall, the Gallery of Honor and the Rembrandt Hall. These rooms are located in the heart of the building on the first floor. More works are on display in the smaller rooms and corridors connecting these three areas.

The Front Hall is the area where Dutch art and history are glorified. Hand-painted decorations on the walls show the beauty and power of nature while tapestries tell stories of important events in Dutch history. The mosaic floor is full of symbols of the four seasons, the galaxy and the star signs. The stained-glass windows are portraits of great musicians, poets and philosophers. Because the decorations are so abundant, it has been decided not to display other objects in this hall.

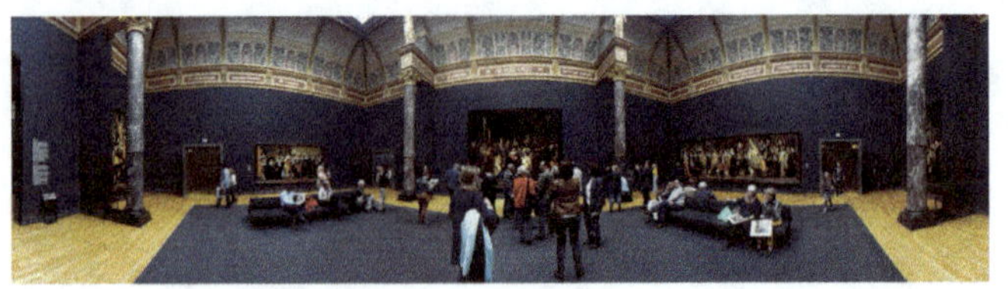

The Gallery of Honor, 2015, Copyright Creative Commons

The Gallery of Honor connecting the Front Hall to the Rembrandt Hall is the heart and soul of the museum. Here you will find the most famous paintings of the Netherlands. If you have limited time, you should definitely visit this gallery.

Designed like the nave of a cathedral, the gallery is a stretched walkway with rooms on either side that serve like little art chapels. Above the side rooms, mural decorations show the arts and crafts of the different provinces of the Netherlands.

The vaults are covered with plants, flowers and petals in paint and stone, while the pillars show various symbols of art and nature.

Apart from *The Night Watch*, the following picture is one of the most popular paintings in the gallery of honor: two lovers in a tender embrace, portrayed by Rembrandt. This painting is known as *The Jewish Bride* but it is probably a portrait of Isaac and Rebecca, taken from the Old Testament. Having to hide their love from others, they act as if they are brother and sister in daily life. When they believe themselves to be unobserved, they can show each other their affection.

Isaac presents his beloved with a golden necklace which he cautiously arranges on her shoulders and chest. While doing so, he slightly touches her left breast. This intimate gesture is answered by Rebecca who puts her fingertips on the back of his hand. Thus, Rembrandt masterfully creates an atmosphere of intimacy and tenderness.

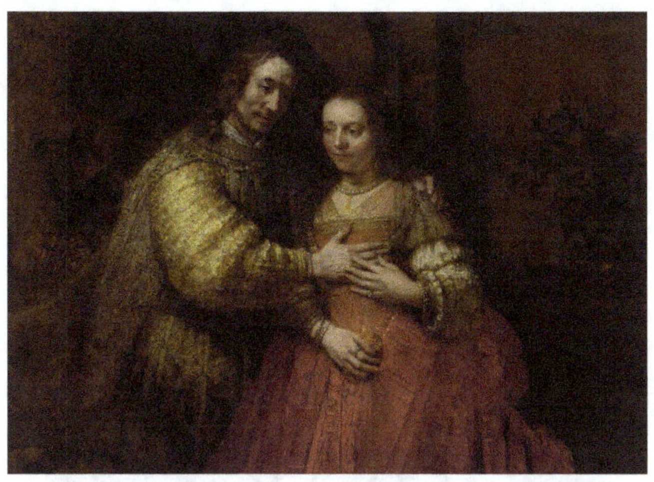

Portrait of a Couple as Isaac and Rebecca, known as 'The Jewish Bride' (circa 1665-circa 1669), Rembrandt van Rijn

The style in which Rembrandt portrayed the couple was modern for its day. In places, the painting looks rather rough and unfinished. Lumps of paint, sometimes put on the canvas with a wooden spatula, literally stick out from the canvas.

Rembrandt painted *The Jewish Bride* late in his career, at a stage when he had freed himself from convention. He moulded his paint, scratched in it and smeared it with a palette knife. The Dutch painter Vincent van Gogh was ecstatic about this work. He was moved by the intimacy of the painting. When van Gogh sat in front of Rembrandt's painting at the opening of the Rijksmuseum in 1885, he did not want to leave. The rough style that the old master used had a strong influence on Van Gogh's own style.

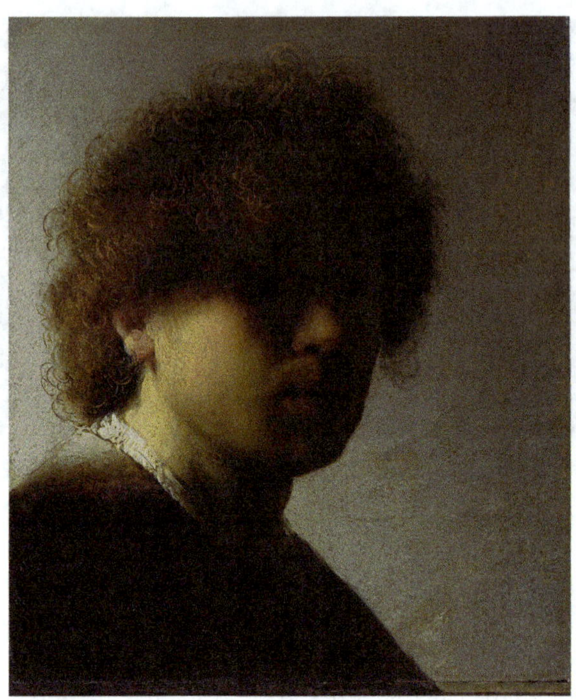

Self-portrait (1628) - Rembrandt van Rijn

This delicate small self-portrait by Rembrandt is a daring masterpiece made at the tender age of twenty-two. The eyes of the artist are almost invisible. If you observe the painting from nearby, you will notice that the curls of his hair are not painted with a brush but have actually been scratched in the still wet paint with the butt end of a brush.

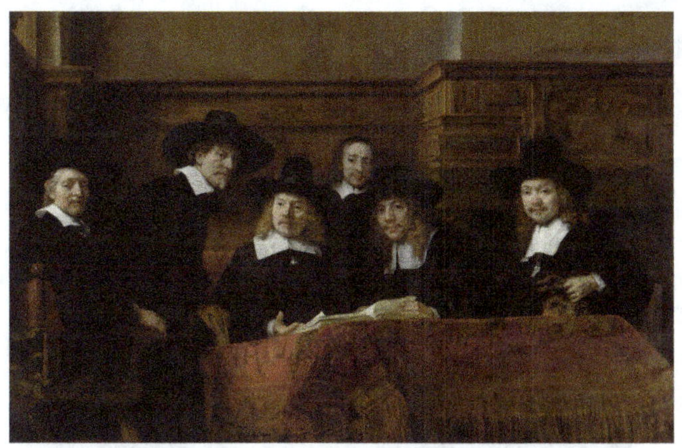

The Syndics of the Drapers' Guild (1662) - Rembrandt van Rijn

When Rembrandt received the commission to portray a group of Amsterdam guild masters, he invented a way to bring some extra life to a potentially static scene of men dressed in black.

It looks as if we, the spectators, burst into the room while the men are still consumed by their work. The men look up as if disturbed. A book with price-lists is still open on the table. The bag of money has not been put away. The second man from the left rises from his seat. Or is he sitting down? We don't know. This way, Rembrandt manages to turn a potentially boring depiction of businessmen at a table into a lifelike and informal scene.

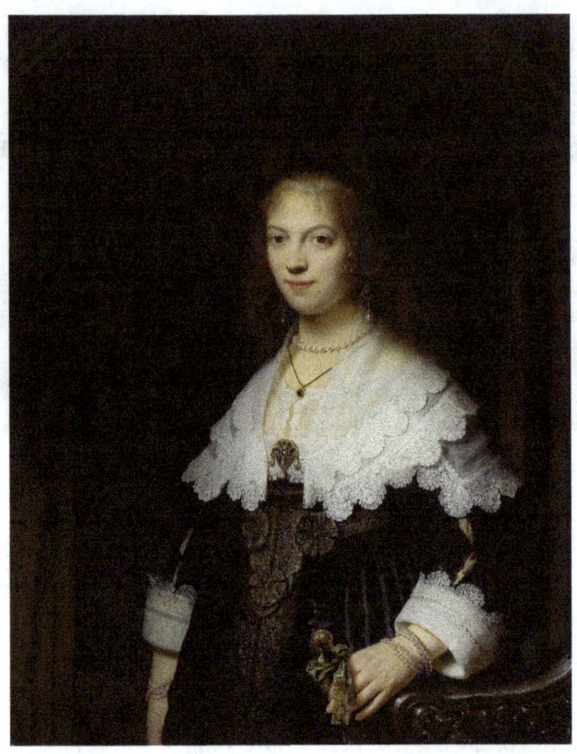

Portrait of Maria Trip (1639) - Rembrandt van Rijn

The young lady in the portrait belonged to the upper class of 17th-century Amsterdam. Her family made a fortune in the weapon and gunpowder trade. She looks us confidently in the eye, and seems to display her wealth with pride.

Everything about her radiates wealth: the fine lace on her shoulders, the pearls, gorgeous ear hangers and the folding fan in her left hand. At the time, this type of fan was a rare and expensive accessory.

Rembrandt made this portrait in 1639, at the peak of his career. With his phenomenal technique and eye for detail, he managed to create an illusion of depth.

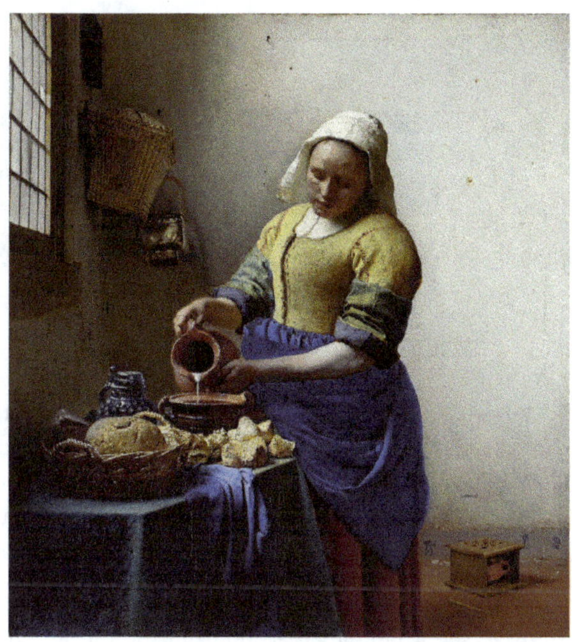

The Milkmaid (circa 1660) - Johannes Vermeer

The Milkmaid is one the most beloved works by Johannes Vermeer of Delft (1632 - 1675). We see a kitchen maid at work who is portrayed with incredible eye for detail.

A basket, pieces of bread and a foot stove on the floor are added to give a glimpse of domestic life in The Netherlands of the 17th century. The girl is a symbol of virtue and obedience. Her tanned arms indicate that she is a servant. Rich people kept their skins pale as a sign of beauty, so pale skin indicated relative wealth and some degree of privilege.

The maid stands still like a statue, and is entirely absorbed in her task, pouring milk into a bowl. She seems to be doing this with great caution. Gluttony was a cardinal sin. The primary colors in her clothes beautifully contrast with the off-white of the wall behind her.

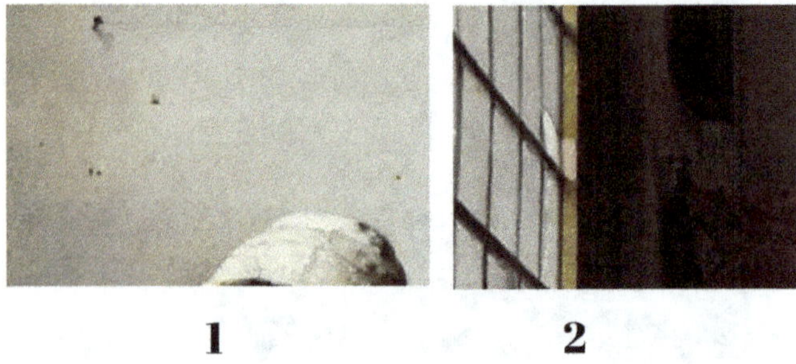

1   2

Please pay special attention to the detail in the background: the scratches on the wall are not cracks in the varnish or paint, but are depictions of actual nail holes (1). If you look at the window on the left, you will notice that a piece of glass is missing (2). The woodwork next to the missing part is somewhat lighter than the rest.

Vermeer's works often have a meditative and enigmatic character. In this delicate painting we see a woman reading a letter, and activity associated with love. The woman may be pregnant but that is not certain, as dresses were supposed to make a woman look full and round. On the table a jewel box refers to vanity.

When you are in the gallery, please have a look at the way Vermeer rendered shadows on the wall. For these shadows the artist used a light blue which was rather innovative for the time.

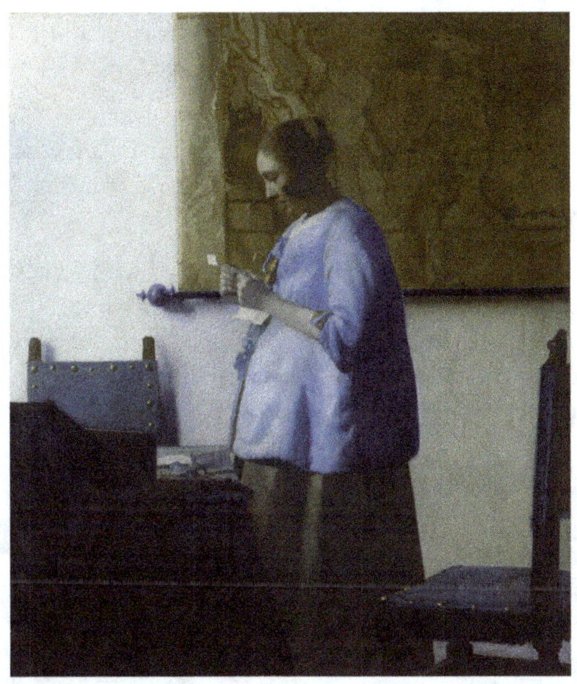

Woman reading a letter (circa 1663) - Johannes Vermeer

Unfortunately Vermeer 's oeuvre is relatively small, consisting only of some thirty paintings. This indicates that he either worked slowly, or that he produced paintings with long intervals in between. The first option seems most likely, given the meticulous attention to detail in his paintings.

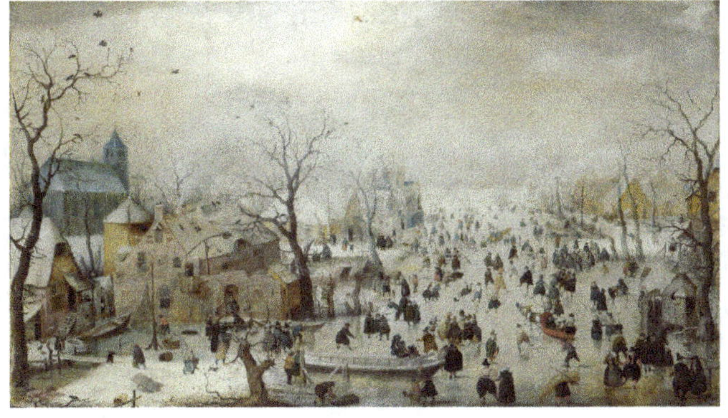

Winter Landscape with Skaters (circa 1608) - Hendrik Avercamp

Apart from soccer, ice-skating is the number one sport in the Netherlands. The country has a lot of waterways and lakes, so there is plenty of opportunity to skate in winter.

Hendrik Avercamp (1585 - 1634) was specialized in winter landscape painting. Being born deaf and mute, drawing and painting were his most important means of communication and expression.

The canvas, with its high vantage point, is packed with little stories. People skate hand in hand, fall flat on their face or play a game of 'kolf', a kind of golf on ice. There is even a horse-drawn sleigh. In the background you can see people dropping their pants to relieve themselves. A couple in love kisses in a haystack.

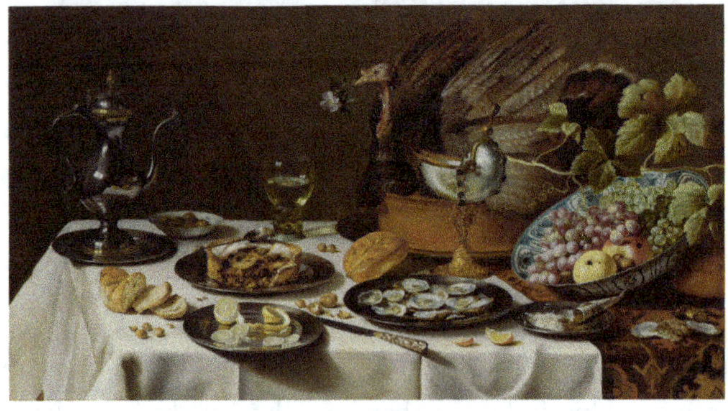

Still-life with Turkey Pie (1627) - Pieter Claesz.

Still-life painting as an independent genre first flourished in the Netherlands during the early 1600s. Still-life paintings were made to educate us. We are all mortal and time passes on. That is why you often find skulls and sandglasses in this genre of painting.

In this particular instance, Pieter Claesz depicted delicious food that is drying out. The technique in *Still-life with Turkey Pie* is breathtaking. Please pay special notice to the way the artist convincingly painted the texture of the nautilus shell and the porcelain blue and white bowl on the right. And when you are in the galleries, try to find the hidden self-portrait of Pieter Claesz. (1596/97 - 1660) in the silver teapot on the left.

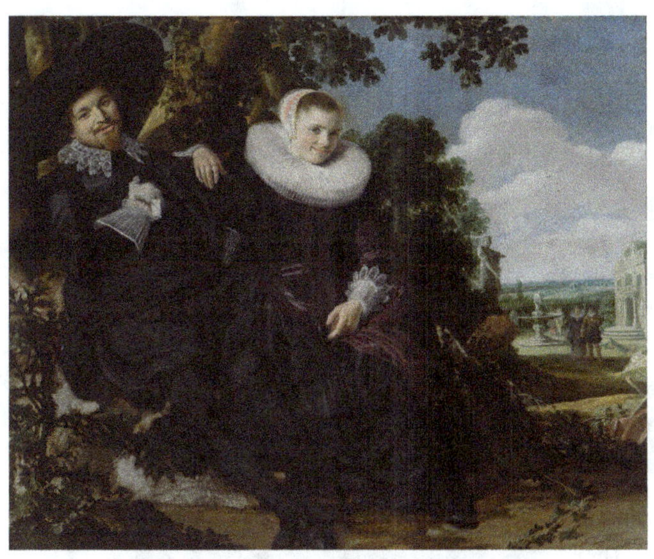

A couple, possibly Isaac Massa and Beatrix van der Laen (circa 1622) - Frans Hals

Frans Hals of Haarlem (1583 - 1666) is known for his loose and virtuoso style. Where other painters reached for perfection in detail, Frans Hals worked with swift brushstrokes, almost nonchalant and carefree. Yet, his paintings look very realistic.

This intimate marriage portrait probably represents the businessman Isaac Massa and his wife Beatrix van der Laen. The couple is surrounded by plants that symbolize virility (the thistle to the man's left) and attachment or affection (the ivy to the woman's right). In the background you can see a garden of love with young couples walking hand in hand.

This painting is a shame-free and happy display of the newlywed's love for each other. At the time, this type of intimacy in portraiture was unusual.

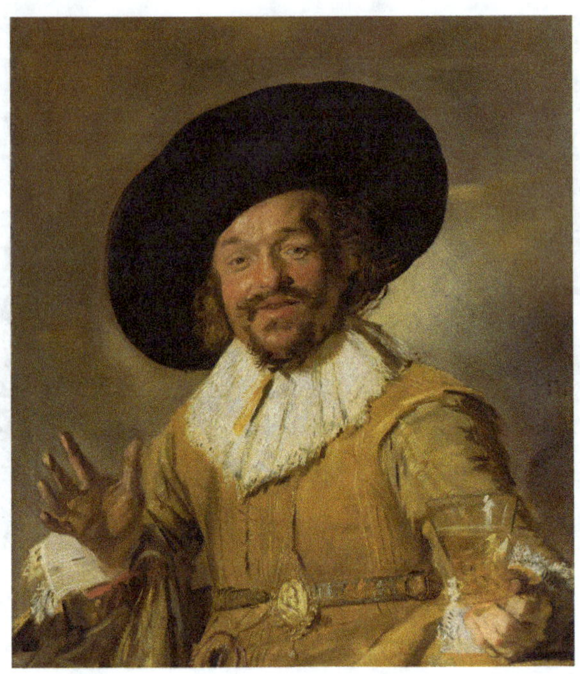

A Militiaman holding a Berkemeyer, also known as 'The Merry Drinker' (circa 1628-1630) - Frans Hals

The Merry Drinker by Frans Hals shows a militiaman holding a glass, a berkemeyer, while he is waving at us with his other hand. His blushing cheeks and slightly tilted posture indicate that this may not have been the first drink of the day. The identity of the man is unknown to us, but does that really matter?

Paintings by Hals are a marvel to look at, both from up close as well as from a long distance. If you observe the painting form up close, you see broad brushstrokes. From a further distance these strokes blend into recognizable shapes. This technique was later used by the Impressionists in the 19th century, and by one famous Frans Hals admirer in particular: Vincent van Gogh.

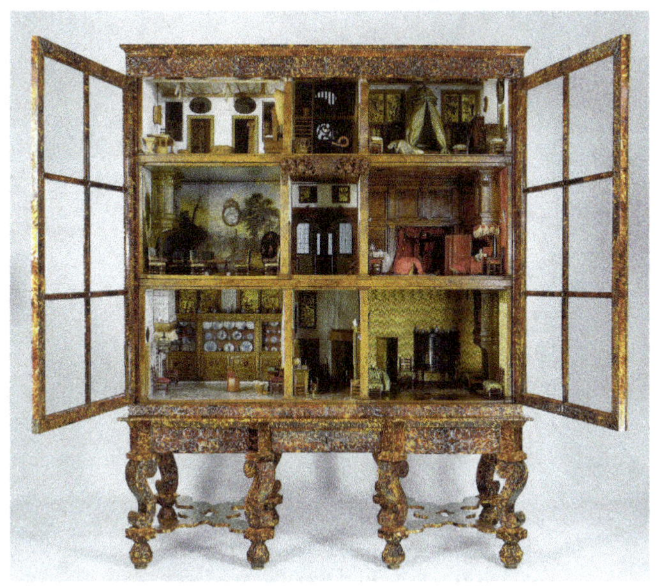

Doll's house of Petronella Oortman, by anonymous artist (circa 1686 - circa 1710)

Doll's houses were the ultimate luxury toy of Amsterdam upper-class ladies. This particular example was already called a 'wonder of the world' at the time. All of its contents were produced with authentic materials, and every piece of furniture and object in the house was copied from real life on a precise scale of 1 to 9.

On the outside, the cabinet is covered with tortoiseshell and pewter inlays. To acquire such a magnificent showpiece, the buyer would pay three times the price of an average canal house in Amsterdam. For art historians and researchers the doll's house is a goldmine of information, showing us exactly how the 17th-century well-to-do decorated their houses.

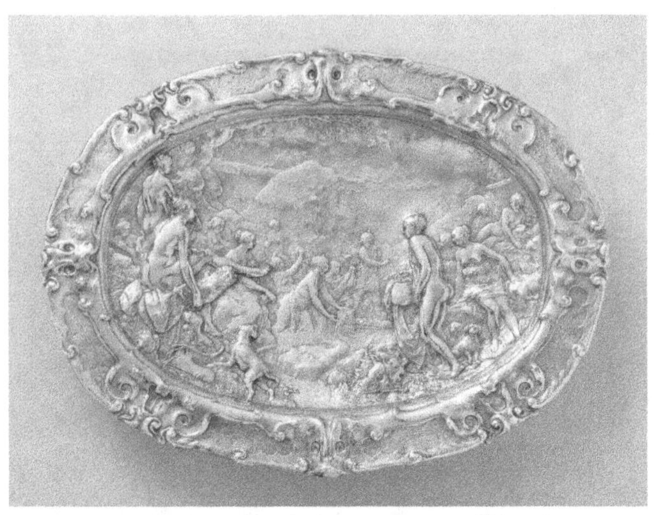

Silver basin with scenes from the story of Diana and Actaeon
(1613) - Paulus Willemsz. van Vianen

This wonderful silver basin depicting a Greek myth is craftsmanship at its highest level, made by the silversmith Paulus Willems. van Vianen (1570 - 1613). You can see Diana and her nymphs taking a bath in the river, at the moment when they are being disturbed by Actaeon. This prince was lost in the forest while hunting.

The punishment for seeing a goddess naked was rather harsh: Actaeon was transformed into a stag and killed by his own friends. This killing scene is depicted on the back of the basin.

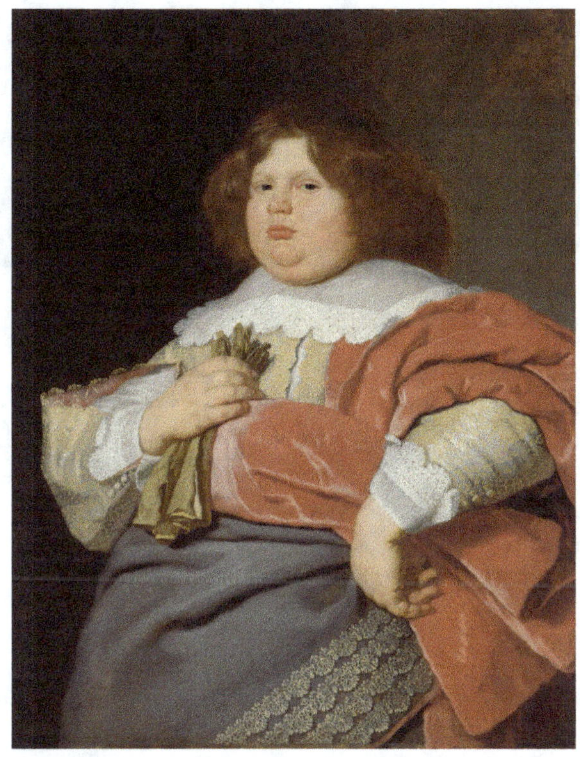

Gerard Andriesz. Bicker (1642) - Bartholomeus van der Helst

The self-assured person in this portrait by Bartholomeus van der Helst is sometimes mistaken by museum visitors to be an angry woman. He is in fact a member of the almighty Bicker family, a clan of businessmen who ruled Amsterdam for nearly 40 years.

The powerful merchants of the city considered themselves the modern version of Roman senators and dressed accordingly in portraits. The gloves in Bicker's right hand signify his sportsmanship, for they are accessories for horseback riding.

Bartholomeus van der Helst (1613-1670) was famous for his expression of textures. By merely looking at his paintings, you can imagine what the textures of the garments must feel like on your skin.

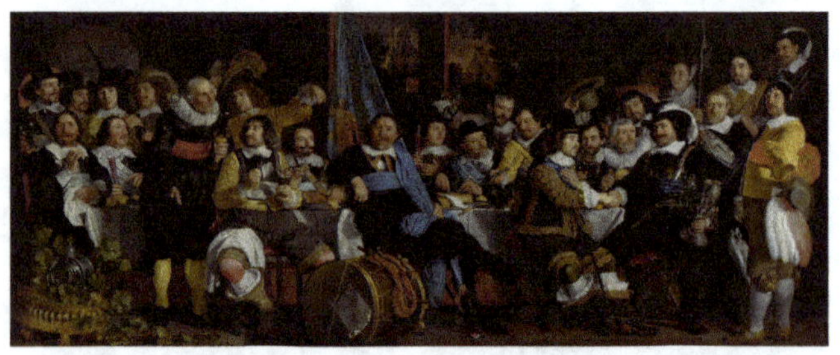

The Guild of St. George, celebrating the Peace Treaty of Munster
(1648) - Bartholomeus van der Helst

The year 1648 is generally considered to be the birth year of the Netherlands as a country. Until then, its provinces had officially been part of the Kingdom of Spain. After the 80-year war against the Spanish King, a peace treaty was signed and the 'Republic of the Seven United Provinces of the Netherlands' was officially acknowledged.

This tiny republic became the center of the world for almost a century. Amsterdam housed the biggest harbor in the world. Shareholding and the stock exchange were invented and Dutch merchants went all over the planet. Colonies were occupied and the town 'New Amsterdam' was founded, the city nowadays known as New York.

The international character of Amsterdam during this Golden Age is visible in the group portrait of the guild of St. George (above). Food and drink were imported from around the world. Red wine came from France and white wine from Germany, olives and lemons were imported from Greece and Italy, the furniture is Italian and the tablecloth was produced in Turkey.

The men seated around the table celebrate the victory over Spain. They eat, drink and shake hands. The flag bearer sits proudly at the center with the banner of Amsterdam wrapped around his shoulders. If you look closely when you are in front of this painting, you will see the famous coat of arms of Amsterdam on the flag: three white crosses on a red and black shield. Also have a look at the silver cup the man in black on the far right is holding. The cup is decorated with a knight on horseback fighting a dragon, while a princess waits to be rescued. This is Saint George, patron saint of this guild. The drum on the floor is silent, indicating that no armies will march to its rhythm anymore. Instead of making noise, the skin of the drum now carries a poem about eternal peace and prosperity.

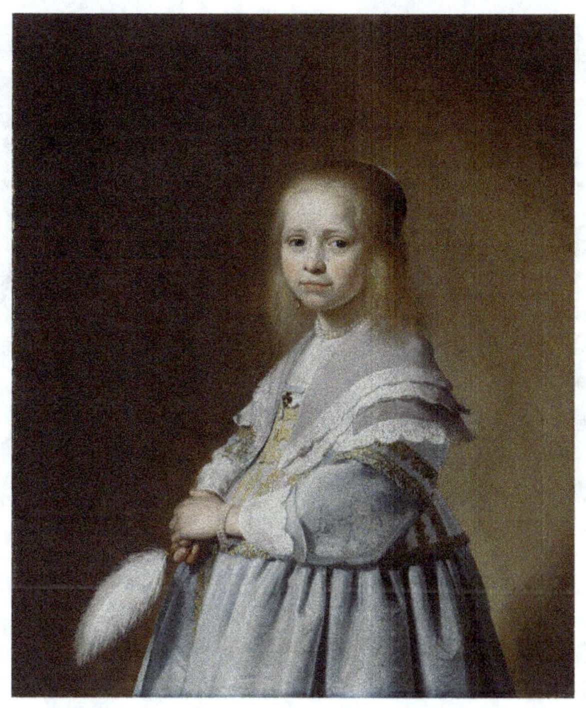

Portrait of a girl in a blue dress (1641) - Johannes Verspronck

In the 17th century, rich children were supposed to dress and behave as adults. It is not known who the girl is in this portrait by Verspronck, but she is obviously from a well-to-do family. Her dress is decorated with gold and lace and she wears pearls around her wrists. An ostrich feather fan in her hand shows her family's delicate taste and wealth. Ostrich feathers were a luxury item at the time.

Portrait of a girl in a blue dress by Johannes Verspronck (1597 - 1662) is popular with both connoisseurs as well as general museum visitors. The look in the girl's eyes is touching; her blushing cheeks and loose hair give her a youthful and innocent appearance.

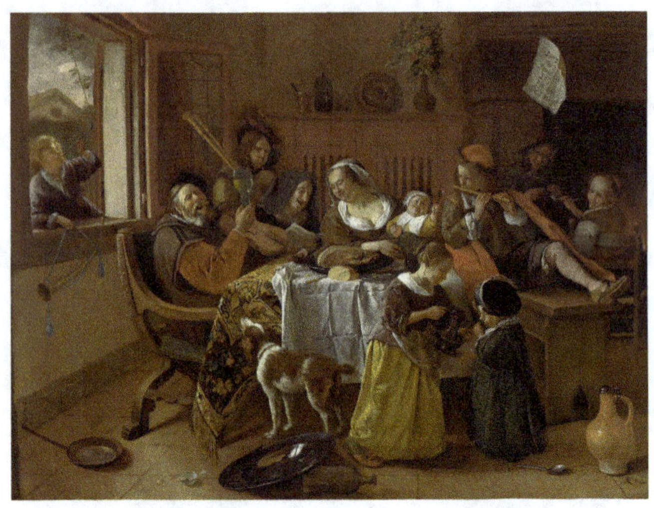

The Merry Family (1668) - Jan Steen

Jan Steen (1625 - 1679) is perhaps the most popular Dutch painter after the 'Big Three', Rembrandt, Vermeer and Frans Hals. Reason for this popularity is Steen's talent to portray lively scenes with people enjoying themselves. He was a born story-teller, which make his paintings a joy to look at.

Although the merry, boisterous family shown here is a great example of this talent, Jan Steen does not promote hedonism and self-indulgence. On the contrary, a painting like this should warn against the dangers of alcohol and lack of self-control.

Looking closely, we see a drunken father singing, the violin slipping from his shoulder. His wife and his mother sing along while a man with bagpipes accompanies them. Nobody seems to be looking after the children, so they make a party of their own, smoking, climbing on the table and drinking. The toddler wearing the green dress gets some wine from his sister.

Over the fireplace at the upper right, a sheet of paper gives away the moral:

'Soo de ouden songen, so pypen de jongen'.

In other words: monkey see, monkey do.

The 18th-century portrait painter Sir Joshua Reynolds, President of the Royal Academy in London, described Jan Steen as follows:

"...if this extraordinary man had had the good fortune to be born in Italy, instead of in Holland, had he lived in Rome instead of Leiden, and been blessed with Michelangelo and Raphael for his masters instead of Brouwer and Van Goyen; the same sagacity and penetration which distinguished so accurately the different characters and expression in his vulgar figures would, when exerted in the selection and imitation of what was great and elevated in nature, have been equally successful; and he now would have ranged with the great pillars and supporters of our Art."

Reynolds was obviously offended by Jan Steen's vulgarity. We now know that Steen's paintings are carefully staged and always carry a moralistic message.

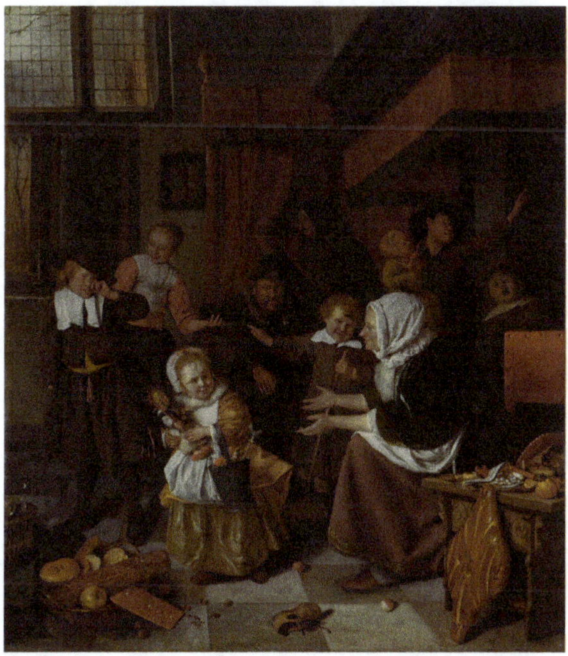

The Feast of St Nicholas (1665-1668) - Jan Steen

Another painting by Jan Steen is this depiction of the feast of St Nicholas. This popular feast has already been celebrated for centuries in the Netherlands. Every year on the 5th of December, good children are rewarded for their behavior and bad children are punished. It is very clear in this painting which child has been good.

The little girl has received a bucket full of sweets and has a doll in her hands. The boy sobs, being teased by his older sister. He did not receive any presents.

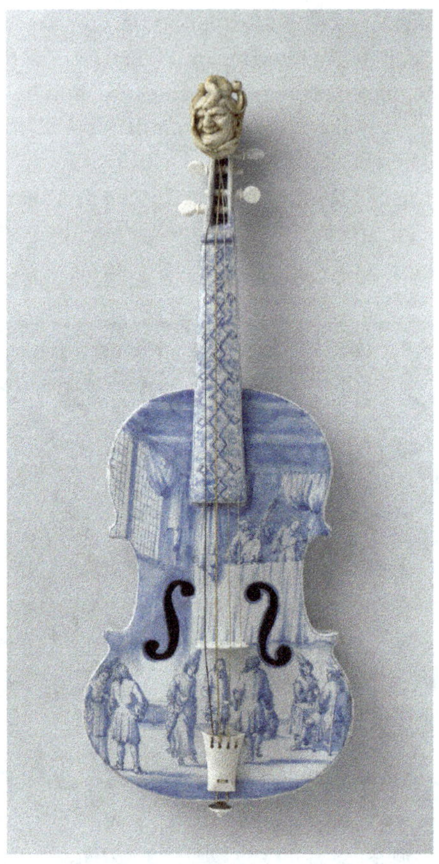

Dutch earthenware violin, by anonymous craftsman (circa 1705 - circa 1710)

Dutch earthenware was originally produced as a cheap copy of refined China porcelain, but soon became a popular item of its own. The texture of Dutch clay does not allow the production of really thin objects, but a Chinese appearance can be faked with glaze. The earthenware is abundantly decorated. The tin-glazed violin shows people dancing to music and playing cards in a public house. It cannot be played; it is a decorative object.

In 1876 the collector John Loudon paid a record 1500 Dutch guilders for this object which was considered to be an exceptional example of Dutch earthenware.

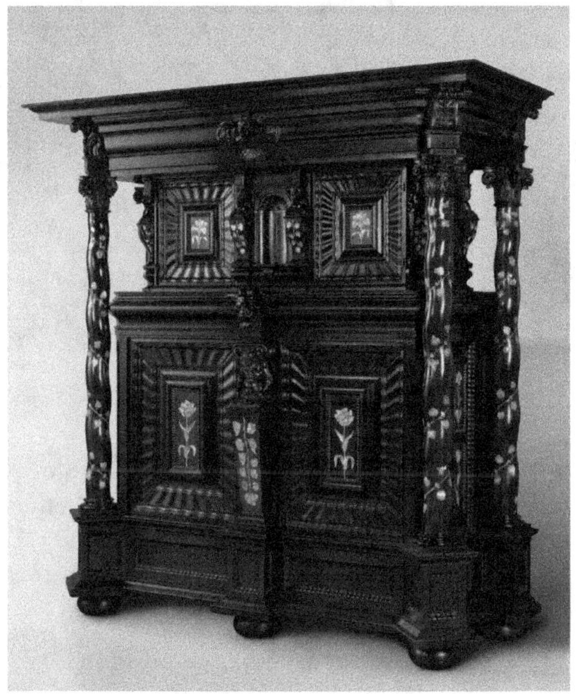

Cupboard (circa 1635 - circa 1645) - Herman Doomer

The rich merchants of Amsterdam did not only show off their wealth with collections of paintings, silver and porcelain, but also with luxurious furniture.

This cupboard was made by Amsterdam's most famous cabinetmaker and ivory carver Herman Doomer (circa 1595 - 1650), using oak and various kinds of exotic wood, such as ebony, rosewood and acacia. The decorations are made of ivory and mother of pearl.

Doomer's workshop also produced picture frames. It is likely that Rembrandt was one of its customers. Rembrandt and Doomer knew each other and Rembrandt painted portraits of the German-born Doomer and his wife. These portraits are at the Metropolitan Museum of Art in New York.

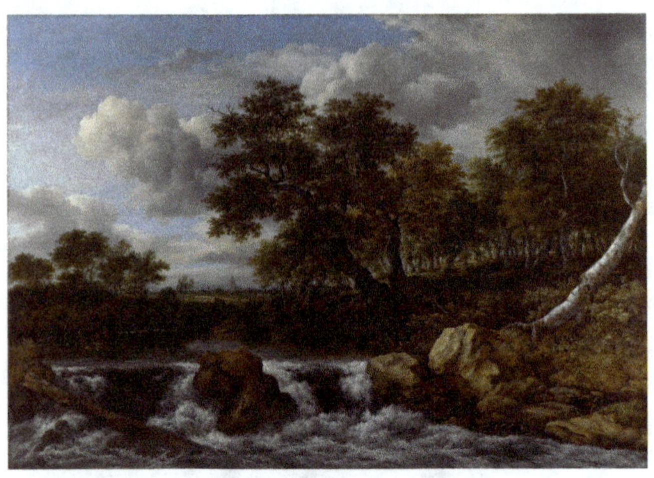

Landscape with waterfall (circa 1668) - Jacob van Ruysdael

Dutch landscape painting became very popular with art lovers in the 17th century. For lack of spectacular mountain ranges in the Netherlands, Dutch painters looked for drama in the depiction of clouds: grey, big and heavy they hang over the landscape. The paintings thus got a theatrical 'larger than life' quality.

Both paintings shown here were made by the artist and doctor Jacob van Ruysdael (1628 - 1682). Interestingly, landscape paintings were not made in the open air. Artists made sketches outdoors and produced the final painting in their workshops, often copying from colleagues.

If you are in the gallery, look for the tiny figures in the grandiose landscape with waterfall. Their small size further enhances the magnificence of nature with its impressive gnarled trees, rolling water and tree trunks.

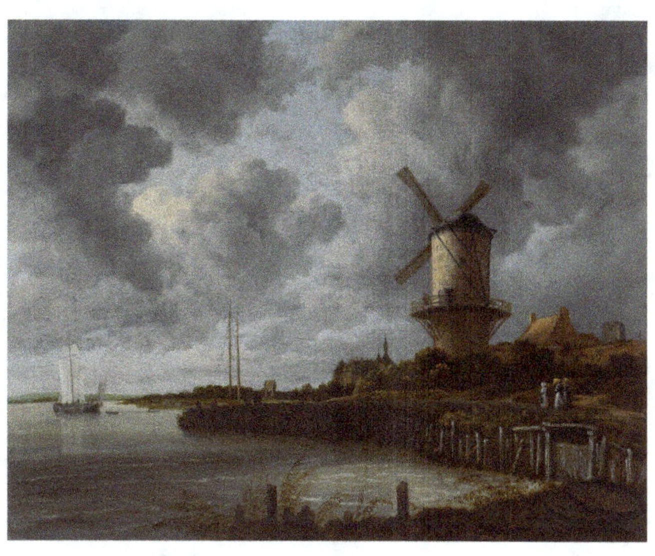

*Windmill at Wijk bij Duurstede (1668-1670) - Jacob van
Ruysdael*

Is there a more typically Dutch landscape than the *Windmill at Wijk bij
Duurstede*? With its majestic windmill, low horizon, broad expanse of the
river and impressive sky with dark rain clouds, there are few paintings more
Dutch than this. One would think that windmills are often depicted in
paintings of the Low Countries, but this is actually one of the few painted
representations of windmills around. The image of the windmill as a typical
feature of the Dutch landscape only came into existence in the 19th
century.

THE REMBRANDT HALL WITH THE NIGHT WATCH

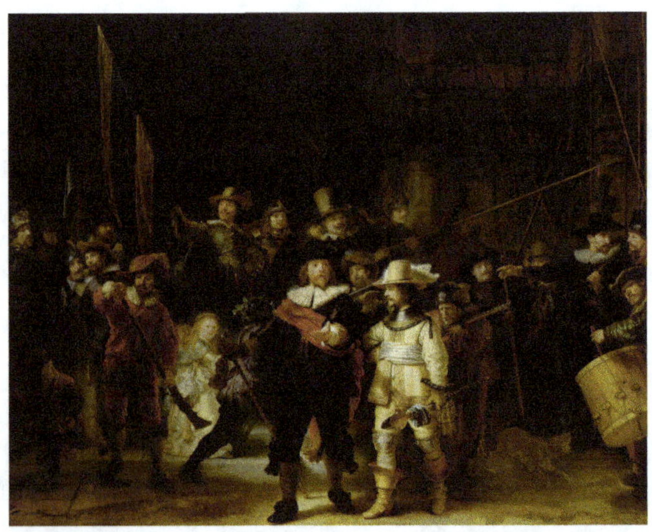

The civic guard of captain Frans Banninck Coq, known as 'The Night Watch' (1642) - Rembrandt van Rijn

At the end of the Gallery of Honor you will find the Rembrandt Hall. This is the most important hall of the Rijksmuseum and entirely dedicated to Rembrandt's masterpiece *The Night Watch*.

In the Republic of the 17th century, the 'burghers' or citizens defended their own cities. The richest businessmen were also the captains of the civic guards. In this painting we see one of those companies, the 'Kloveniers', set off to march.

The painting is an incredible display of movement and light. Nobody poses for the painter but all the men march, talk, prepare their guns or wave a flag. A little girl carrying a dead chicken runs into the scene. A young boy carries the gunpowder for the soldier charging his gun on the left. The drummer starts beating the rhythm to which the soldiers will march.

The painting is a snapshot. With his famous use of light effects, Rembrandt created a scene that is almost three-dimensional. The figures are life-size and move informally and naturally. It was already very popular to be portrayed in a slightly informal and relaxed manner, but Rembrandt perfected this. The result is astonishingly realistic. Pay special attention to these details when you are standing in front of *The Night Watch*.

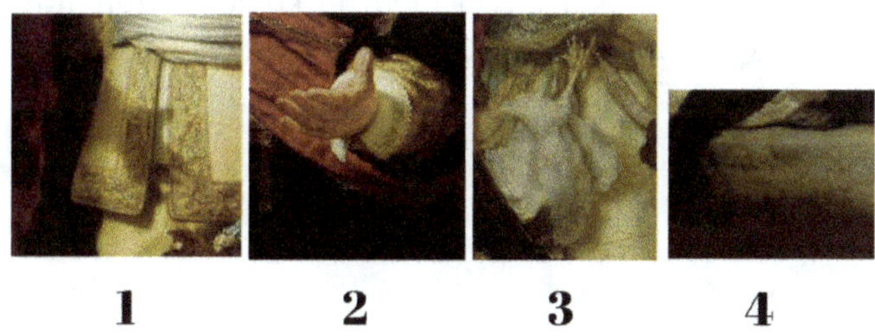

1   2   3   4

The 3D-effect: The outstretched arm of the captain in the center casts a shadow (1) on the yellow tunic of his lieutenant. The open hand (2) catches the sunlight and seems to stick out of the canvas. The yellow uniform and white scarf are painted with microscopic detail.

The shadow of the hand 'grips' a lion standing on its hind feet in the embroidery of the uniform. The lion holds a shield with three crosses on it: the coat of arms of Amsterdam. With minuscule brushstrokes Rembrandt depicts the embroidery in full detail.

Behind the captain a small soldier fires a gun. Only his curved leg and his shining helmet are visible. The helmet is adorned with oak leaves, the symbol of victory.

Left, we see a girl with a chicken on her belt. The chicken's feet ('clauwe')

(3) symbolise the army of 'clauweniers' ('Kloveniers'). The girl resembles Rembrandt's first wife Saskia, but it is not 100% certain it is her. Under her foot the painter signed '*Rembrandt f(ecit) 1642*' (4).

The location of the painting in the museum building is symbolic. The museum itself has been designed like a cathedral, with the Gallery of Honor being the nave and the rooms around the gallery serving as chapels. The Rembrandt Hall is located where in a cathedral one would find the altar. It is therefore the most 'sacred' place of the building.

The center of this hall is of course *The Night Watch* itself, but there is more. The decorations in the Rembrandt Hall around this painting are glorifications of the painter's life and works. Standing on separate columns, statues with veils symbolize the four periods of the 24-hour cycle: Evening, Night, Morning and Day. The darker the moment of the day, the more the statues cover their faces.

Rembrandt was the master of light and dark, all different light tones are present. Rembrandt's life story is painted in golden letters over the dark walls. The ceiling is covered with symbols of nature, just like in the Front Hall and the Gallery of Honor.

MEDIEVAL AND 16TH-CENTURY ART

The Rijksmuseum has combined its objects of medieval and Renaissance art in one exhibition. You will find this section in the basement of the building.

Dutch history is not particularly well-known for its medieval and Renaissance art. The more famous developments in art and science in the Netherlands took place after that period, in the 17th century, the Golden Age. The centuries preceding this blooming period are less well-known, which is unjustified. It is a rich age with some exceptionally beautiful objects and paintings.

The central subject in this exhibition is religion. In the Middle Ages, religion is everywhere in daily life. Christianity is a world power with political influence. Churches are the most important and visible buildings in every European city.

The objects of the medieval art section tell the stories of the lives of Jesus, Mary and Joseph, as well as biblical tales with a moral. Various saints are represented by statues and relics. Religious objects were made for use in public spaces like churches and town halls but also for private use in a domestic setting.

The art works of the 16th century show a shift towards a more human-centered world. Individualism results in the production of self-portraits and the depiction of real people. Interest in ancient cultures becomes visible by depictions of Venus and other pagan figures. We also see developments in style and technique. Objects become more realistic, and the human figure is rendered with more movement. Influence from Italian artists is recognizable in perspective, volume and a more lifelike depiction of the human body.

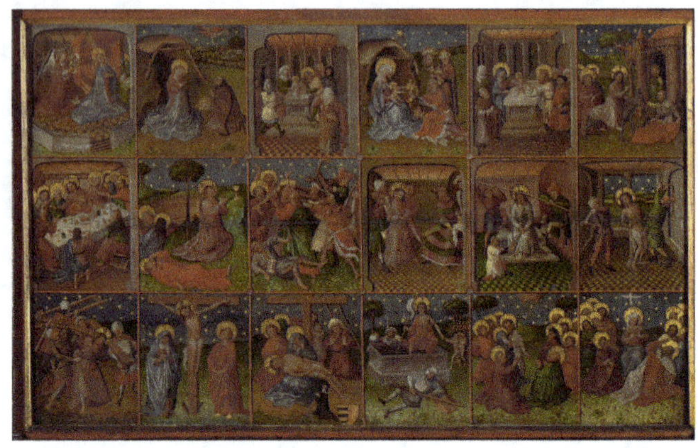

Scenes from The Life of Christ, *by anonymous artist, circa 1435*

The first object you should take some time for is this depiction of the life of Christ. One could call it a 15th-century cartoon strip, displaying all the important scenes from the Gospel. It was made in a century when reading and writing were exclusively the domain of the nobility and the clergymen. Ordinary people could learn about Jesus and other biblical stories by studying panels, sculptures and stained glass windows. Like a Marvel Comic this panel shows us the life and works of Jesus Christ, from the Annunciation of Mary at the top left to the Messiah's crucifixion and resurrection at the lower right.

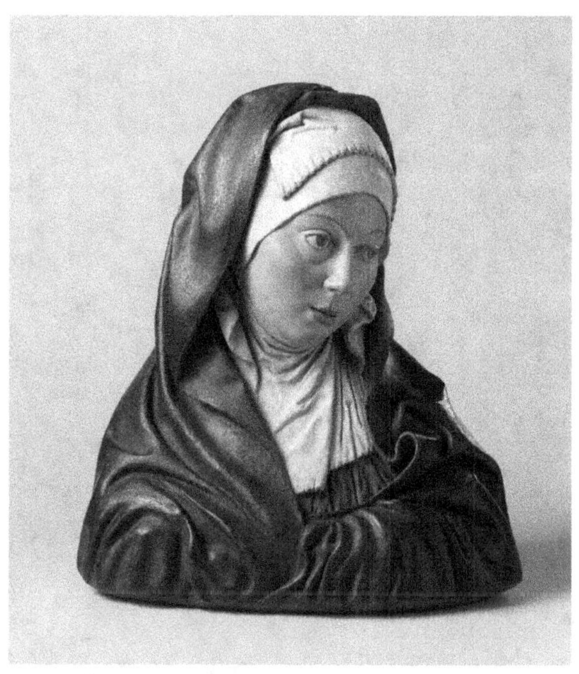

The Virgin as Mater Dolorosa (Our Lady of Sorrows), (circa 1507 - circa 1510), attributed to Pietro Torrigiani

This terra-cotta bust of a weeping woman represents Mary, the mother of Jesus. People in the Middle Ages would immediately recognize her by the blue and white garment. This is the only known bust of this type in the Netherlands.

Her slightly tilted head testifies to the grief of the *Mater Dolorosa*, the Lady of Sorrows, crying at the foot of the cross where her son had died. Without extreme facial expressions or postures, her grief is shown with restraint and cool.

Traditionally, one could encounter a crying Mary in paintings rather than in sculptures. It is a good example of the Northern European style. The bust has been attributed to Pietro Torrigiani, an Italian living in Bruges where he was in the service of the Archduchess Margaret of Austria. For the Archduchess the subject of a grieving female was particularly relevant since she was a grieving widow herself.

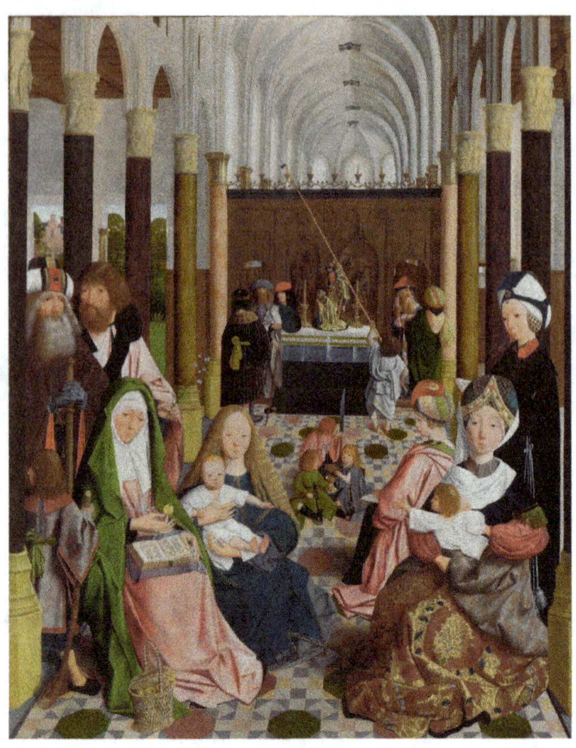

The Holy Kinship (circa 1494) - (workshop of) Geertgen tot Sint Jans

The Holy Family consisted of nineteen people. In this painting we see all of them together, set in an imaginary medieval church. Mary in the blue dress with Jesus on her lap modestly sits just left of the center. Her mother Anne sits nearby, holding a book. Behind them on the left, we see their husbands Joseph and Joachim. The two figures on the right are Mary's cousin Elizabeth who is holding her son, John the Baptist, on her lap. John the Baptist points his little finger at Jesus. In the background we see Mary's sisters accompanied by their husbands and children.

It is a wonderfully detailed painting. Take a closer look at the golden statue on the altar, representing Abraham sacrificing Isaac. The screen behind the altar shows the origin of worldly sin: the temptation of Eve by the snake and the expulsion from Paradise. John the Baptist in the foreground points at Jesus: 'He is our Saviour'. These elements foretell the sacrifice that Jesus will make years later to relieve the world from its sins.

Another detail worthwhile observing: some parts of the painting have been restored. The difference between the original painting and modern retouches is visible. Look for the thin grey lines in the colors.

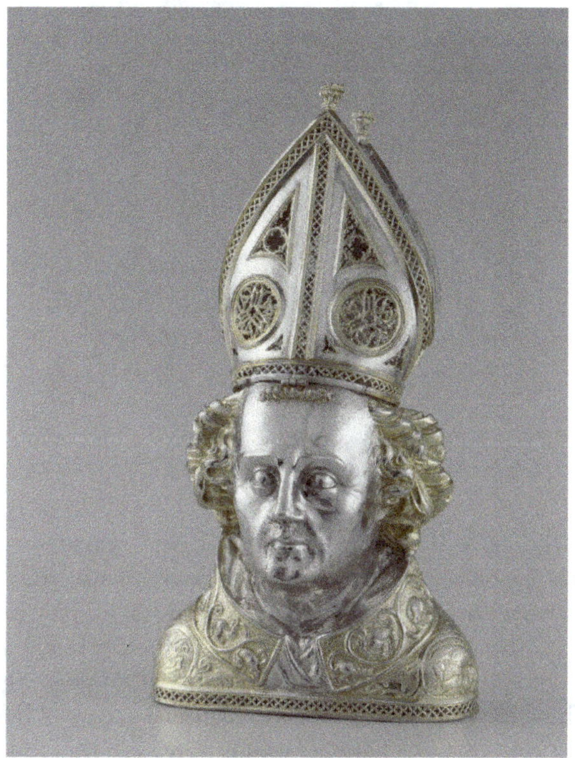

Bust of Saint Frederic (1362) - Elias Scerpswert

This silver bust is both a reliquary and a portrait of Saint Frederic of Utrecht. Once it contained part of the skull of this holy bishop who got murdered in 838 AD. On holidays, the bust would be shown to the people together with the skull fragment.

Unlike other busts where saints are depicted with almost abstract features, this particular example is more lifelike. Frederic has wrinkles in his face, stubbles and a balding crest. The silver bust is known as a 'speaking reliquary'. Underneath his body a silver plate is added with the inscription:

'The dean and chapter of the Salvator Church [...] had me exhumed in 1362 AD [...]'

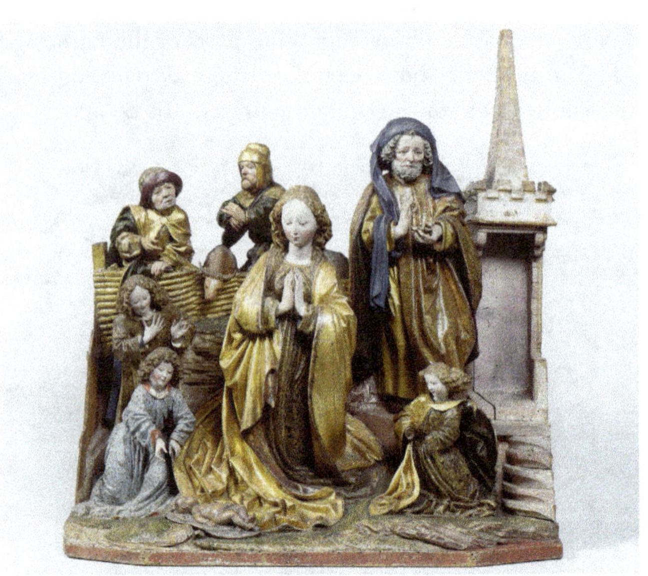

The Nativity (circa 1470) - attributed to Hans Kamensetzer

Throughout the ages, the representation of the Christmas story and its characters has become more and more 'ordinary', with lifelike figures. In this gracious wooden nativity group we see Mother Mary praying, while baby Jesus is lying on a fold of her mantle. Joseph holds a candle and protects the flame from the wind. Shepherds and singing angels complete the scene. The artist who carved this set has been successful in rendering an elegant, realistic group of convincing proportions.

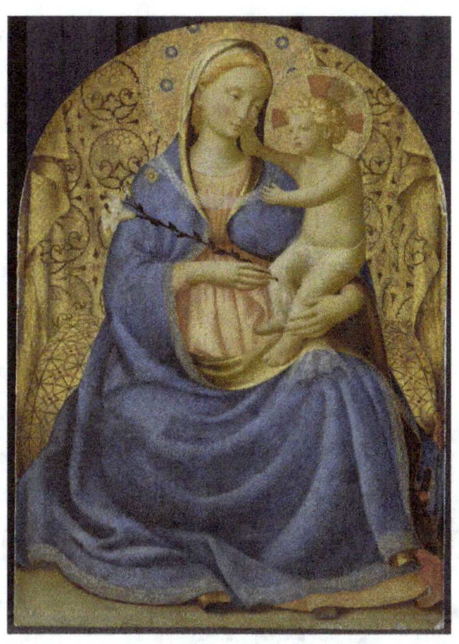

Madonna of Humility, Fra Angelico, circa 1440

This depiction of the Madonna with Jesus was made by the famous monk and painter from Florence, Fra Angelico (1400 - 1469). Since Mary is seated on a cushion and not on a throne she symbolizes humility and approachability.

The halos around their heads, decorated with punched circles and without perspective, are typical of the style of Fra Angelico.

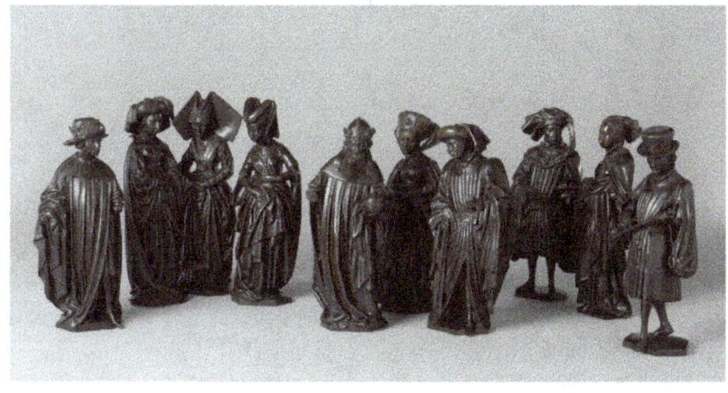

Mourners as decoration of the tomb of Isabella of Bourbon (1476) - attributed to) Jan Borman (?) and (attributed to) Renier van Thienen

These sculptures are so-called 'pleurants' or 'weepers', and once decorated the tomb of Isabelle of Bourbon who died at the age of twenty-nine in 1465. All figures represent family members or ancestors. Only ten out of the original number of 24 weepers have survived.

Mourning was a strict ritual in which everyone played a specific role. Public display of emotions was frowned upon. One had to keep his posture and express grief in a controlled manner. Therefore the figures are solemn and pensive.

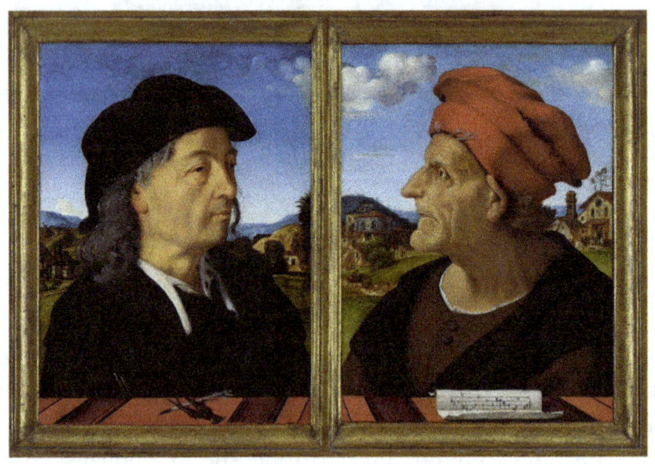

Giuliano and Francesco da Sangallo (circa 1482-85) - Piero di Cosimo

In the Renaissance, mankind shrugged off anonymity. God and the saints were no longer the only subjects of art. Recognizable, 'real' people took to the stage, showing their name, profession and status.

This double portrait is a great example. On the left we see the architect Giuliano da Sangallo, the master builder of St. Peter's basilica and good friend of Michelangelo.

A pair of compasses and a pen in front of him represent his métier. The man on the right is Giuliano's father, the architect and composer Francesco Giamberti da Sangallo. His occupation is symbolised by a sheet of music. In the background our eyes can dwell on a delightful Tuscan landscape.

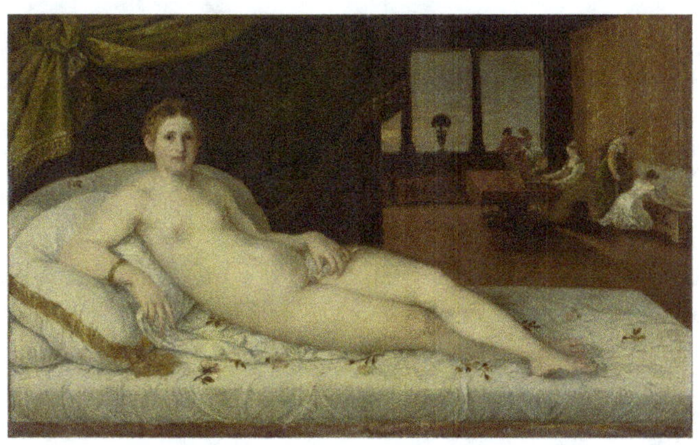

Lying Venus (circa 1540-1560) - Lambert Sustris

The Dutch painter Lambert Sustris (circa 1515 - after 1568) was one of the close collaborators of the Venetian master Titian (1487 - 1567), whose *Venus of Urbino* he copied.

Whereas a goddess was usually portrayed as unapproachable and distant, the Amsterdammer Sustris placed the nude Venus in an informal setting, a Renaissance residence with employees working in the background, thereby making her more human.

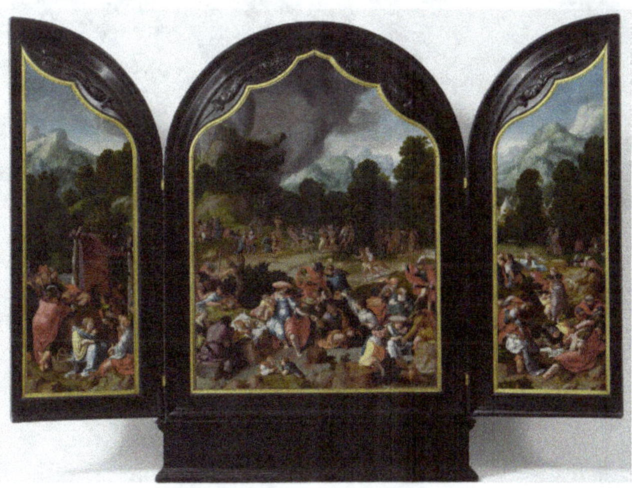

The Adoration of the Golden Calf (circa 1530) - Lucas van Leyden

41

This triptych, showing the adoration of the golden calf as described in the book Exodus, is full of movement and a feast for the eyes. Having lost their faith in God, the Israelites created their own idol to worship. They lost their decency and morality and started drinking, partying and making love in the open. Yahweh was very angry that the Israelites had made the Golden Calf and that they were adoring another god. Moses had all of them killed.

It contains wonderful details depicting debauchery: the drinking, the puking and the dancing. One woman looks us right in the eye, as if to invite us to join in. Everywhere you look, you see skin and shapes of fleshy bodies, belly buttons and butt cheeks. In the middle panel a woman in a blue dress offers an apple to a man next to her. It is the fall into sin all over again.

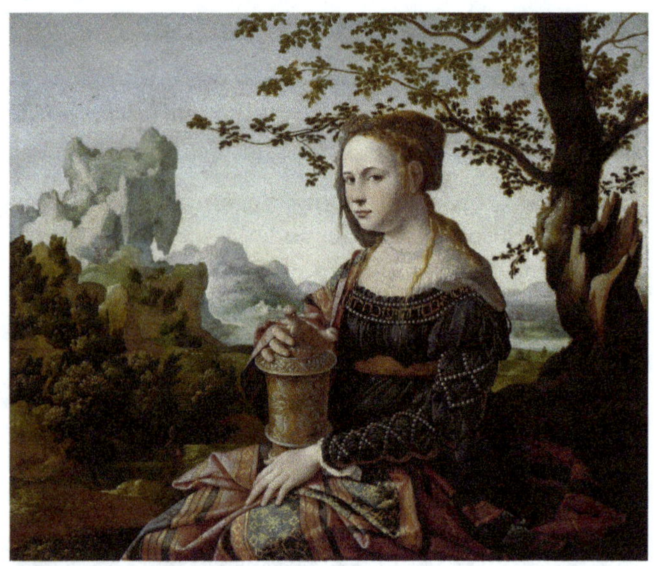

Mary Magdalene (circa 1530) - Jan van Scorel

In this picture by Jan van Scorel (1495 - 1562), Mary Magdalene is portrayed holding the pot containing the ointment for Jesus' feet. She is elegantly dressed, referring to her past as a high-class prostitute.

In the background the painter depicted her a second time. According to legend, after Jesus' death she lived as a hermit for the rest of her life. Every day, angels would lift her up and show her future life in heaven. Almost invisible (surely in this book, but even in real life), that scene is depicted against the rocks in the distance.

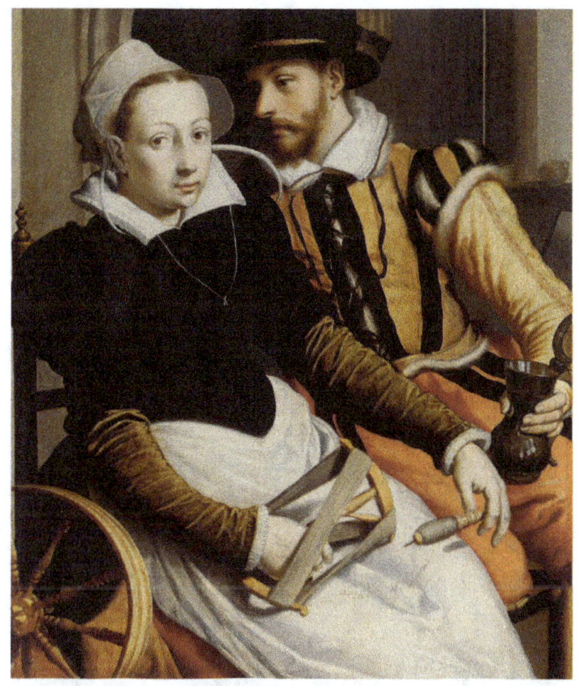

Man and Woman at a Spinning Wheel (circa 1565) - Pieter Pietersz.

The scene in this painting is what we can call a 'cliffhanger'. A woman at a spinning wheel is interrupted by a man offering her a drink. She looks at the spectator, as if to ask us what to do. We will never know her decision.

Even though the Church's influence on everyday life weakened in the Renaissance, painters like Pieter Pietersz. (circa 1541 - 1603) still added morality to their works. Virtue versus sin, pleasure versus discipline. If you compare this work with medieval paintings, you see a distinct development. Now, there is volume, perspective and refinement.

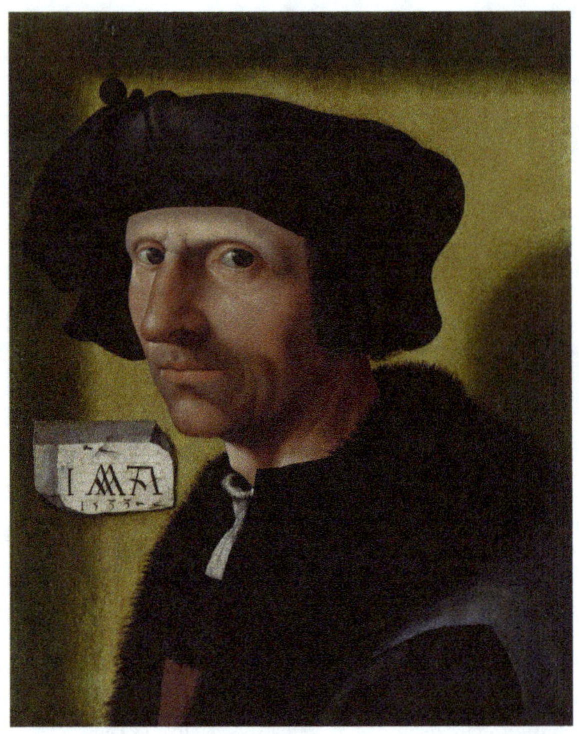

Self-portrait (circa 1533) - (workshop of) Jacob Cornelisz. Van Oostsanen

This bust-length painting is often considered to be the oldest known self-portrait in the Netherlands. The original must have been older but is unknown to us. The painting in the Rijksmuseum, made on a plank, in all likelihood is a copy.

The painter depicted is Jacob van Oostsanen (circa 1472 - 1528), who shows his social status and self-confidence by portraying himself as a well-dressed man who looks us right in the eye. He is wearing a black bonnet with earflaps, and a fur-trimmed dark gown over a white shirt with a gathered collar and a red jacket.

In the Renaissance, artists were more than just craftsmen working for the Church or the King. They were individuals with a soul and a voice, and their own signature, both literally and figuratively. On the sheet of paper on the wall he wrote his initials **I W** (inverted) v **A**.

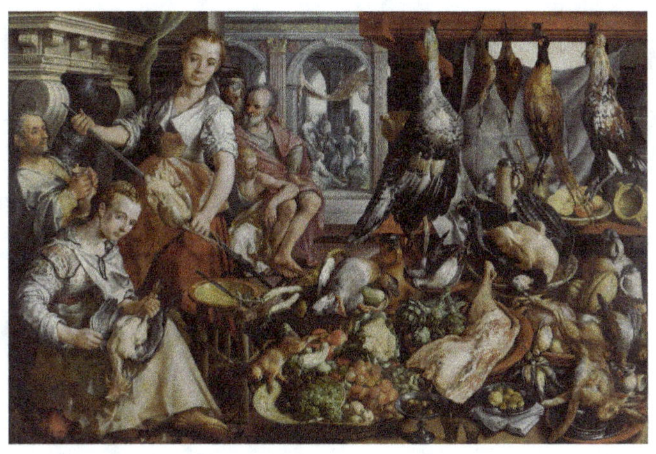

The well-stocked Kitchen (1566) - Joachim Bueckelaer

The kitchen in this painting shows us wealth and abundance, displaying meat, poultry, vegetables and exotic food everywhere. There are jars and plates and two women preparing a chicken dish. It may look like an invitation to enjoy life's delights, there is a catch. The subject of this painting is not about a display of food and abundance. Just have a look at the background and you will see Jesus visiting the two sisters Mary and Martha. That is the real subject of the painting, while the artist used the kitchen setting as an excuse to paint food and objects.

In the original Bible story Mary sits and listens to Jesus' teachings, while Martha gets up and prepares dinner. Jesus tells them that Mary's way is the right way to react. She does not care about worldly matters, but sits still to focus on the spiritual message.

"As Jesus and his disciples were on their way, he came to a village where a woman named Martha opened her home to him. She had a sister called Mary, who sat at the Lord's feet listening to what he said. But Martha was distracted by all the preparations that had to be made. She came to him and asked, "Lord, don't you care that my sister has left me to do the work by myself? Tell her to help me!" "Martha, Martha," the Lord answered, "you are worried and upset about many things, but few things are needed —or indeed only one. Mary has chosen what is better, and it will not be taken away from her."

Between background and foreground there is a third element: old men dressed like Romans, presumably discussing, symbolizing virtue.

This kind of rhetoric is often used in 16th-century art. The combination of everyday life in the present with an age-old message from the Bible.

The painter is Joachim Bueckelaer (1533 - 1575), whose 'kitchen scenes' were popular at the time.

18TH-CENTURY ART

The 18th century is the age of refinement. The Netherlands have lost their position as a leading world power but are still a rich country. Families who made their fortune in the Golden Age spend their money on art.

As you will see in this section of the Rijksmuseum, the 18th-century upper class turns its houses into artworks as a whole. Whereas the 17th-century elite would simply decorate their walls with paintings, that did not do for the generations after them. Having your own art collection in a beautiful house is a matter of prestige. Knowledge of and love for music, literature and visual arts are all part of one's status.

The main influence on these developments is the royal court in France. The Dutch imitate French fashion by wearing wigs and costumes of the nobility. Houses and gardens are designed in the French style, and people speak French. Therefore, this is not an 'exclusively Dutch' exhibition, like in the 17th-century section.

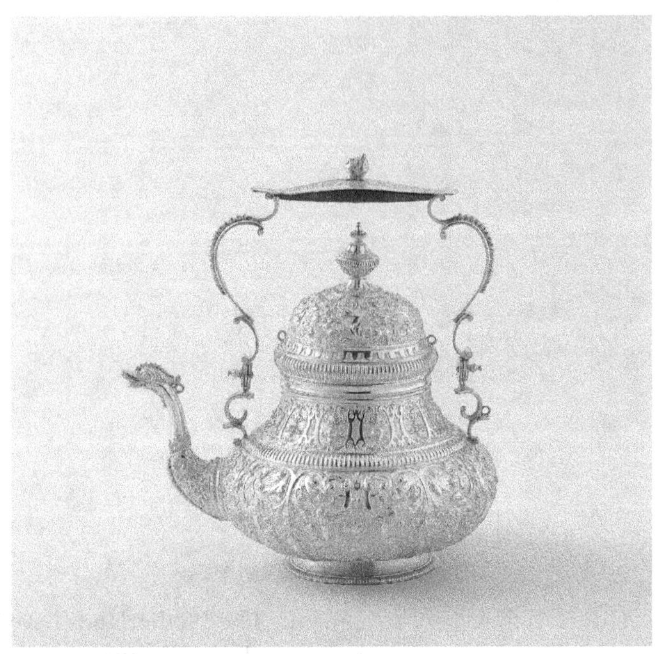

Tea kettle (1738) - Gabijnus van der Lely

An important part in this lifestyle is played by a particular room in the 18th-century house, the Salon. Here one can lavish his wealth and good taste on his visitors. It is the room to discuss politics, art and science. Concerts take place in the Salon as well as lectures, debates and card games. Tea and wine are served in elegant silver and porcelain sets. Household objects are turned into art, the beginning of 'applied arts'.

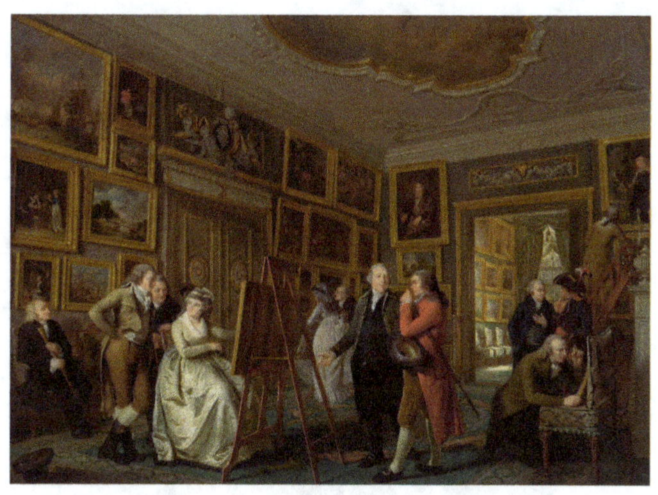

The Art Gallery of Jan Gildemeester (circa 1794 - 1795) -
Adriaan de Lelie

The merchant Jan Gildemeester bought a luxurious canal house on Herengracht in Amsterdam in 1792. Two rooms of this house were decorated as an art gallery, with paintings hanging frame to frame. Modern museums still had to be invented. For a long time, art collections were a personal business.

Jan Gildemeester is portrayed in the middle, wearing a blue and gray suit. He is in conversation with an man in a red jacket. The other visitors take their time to look at the paintings in the room.

The scene is informal and relaxed. Not only can we admire the painter Adriaan de Lelie (1755 - 1820) for his technique, we also get a glimpse on what the art lovers of the 18th century collected.

By observing the painting closely, you can recognize the works on the wall. The gentleman standing on the stairs in the background on the right is studying *Man With Falcon* by Rubens up close. Over Jan Gildemeester's head we see Rembrandt's *Preacher*. Also visible are landscapes by Ruysdael and Hobbema and paintings by Metsu, Dou and Terborch.

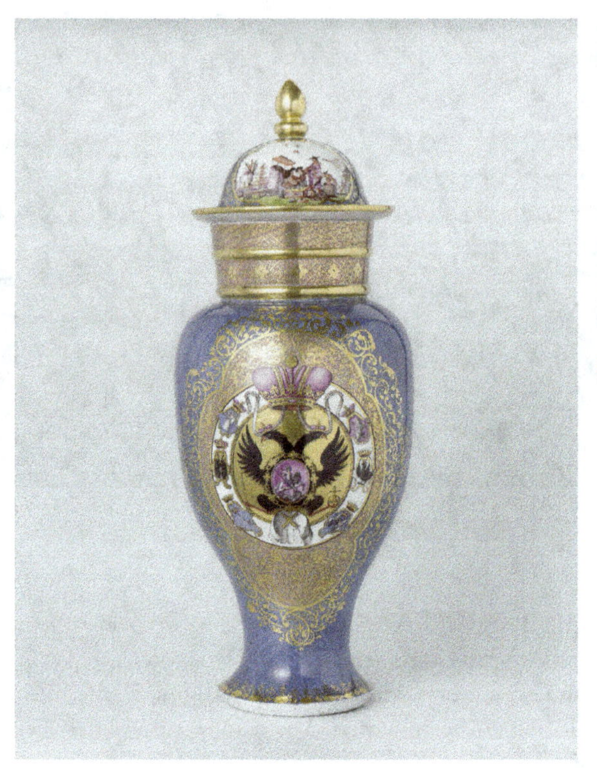

Lidded vase with gold paint (1727)

This blue vase is one of the top pieces of the Meissen collection in the Rijksmuseum. It has been lavishly decorated with gold paint and mother of pearl glaze.

On the lid we see a so-called 'chinoiserie': a Chinese-looking decorative element. The Russian coat of arms has been painted onto the vase itself; in 1728 August the Strong sent this vase as a gift to the Russian court.

Until the 18th century, porcelain was exclusively a Chinese or Japanese product. The mineral kaolin, essential for making porcelain because of its fine structure, was only found there. When kaolin was also discovered near the German town of Meissen at the beginning of the 18th century, it kickstarted the European porcelain production.

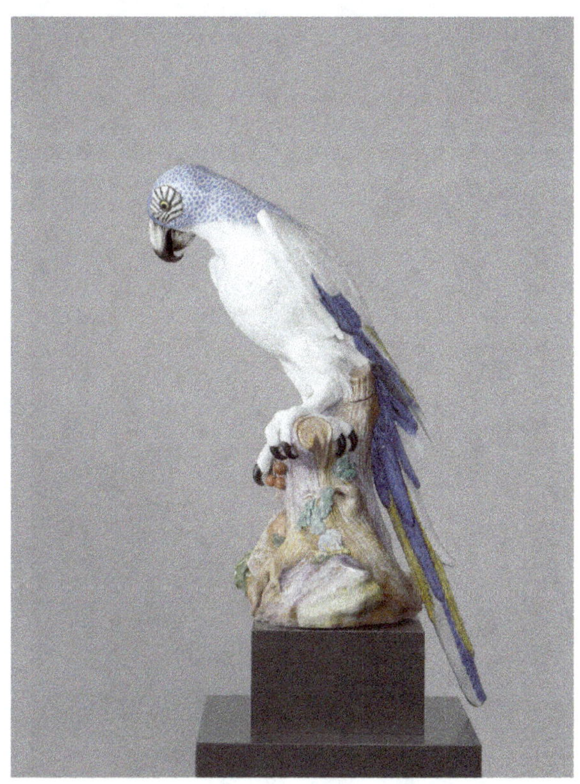

Blue Macaw - Meissener Porcelain Manufactur (1731)

This porcelain bird was owned by the Elector of Saxony, August the Strong (1670 - 1733), a lover of birds. His two passions, porcelain and exotic animals, were combined in the many animal figures that decorated the walls of his palace in the Japanese style.

If you look closely at the bird when you are in the gallery, you will notice that it has been painted over, but not entirely. This way, there is visible proof that the object is really made of porcelain.

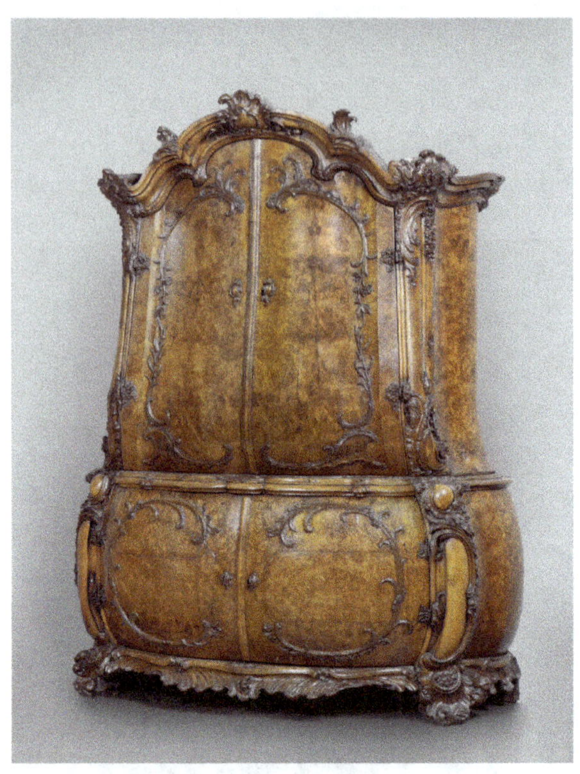

Cabinet in rococo style (circa 1755-1765)

This oak cabinet is a great example of the so-called 'rococo' style: curved shapes and asymmetric floral ornaments. The cabinet has not one straight line in it, everything is curved. The decorative elements are shaped like leaves, which is typical for the era. Even the keyholes are surrounded by decorations. One could view it as as a piece of sculpture rather than as a cabinet.

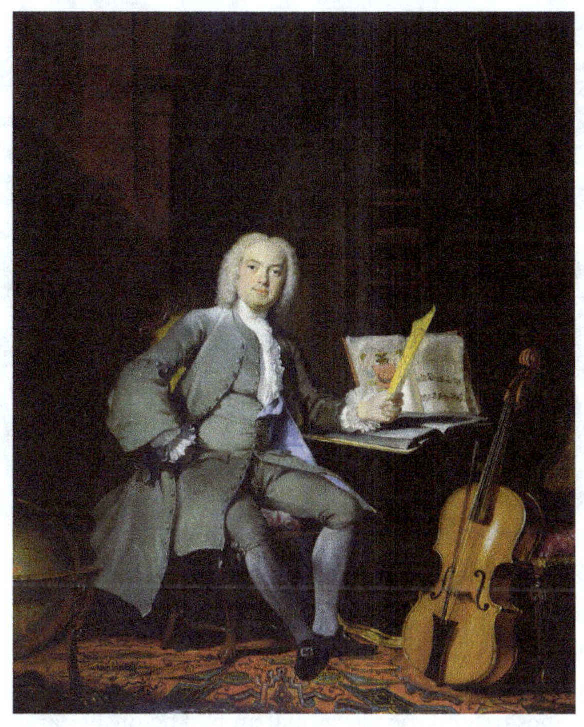

A member of the Van Mersch Family (1736) - Cornelis Troost

This is the ultimate 18th-century gentleman. Dressed in the latest French fashion and wearing a wig, he sits comfortably in his study, showing us his wealth and education.

Everything in the room around the sitter suggests refinement. The book on the table and the cello testify to his love for music, the globe on the left to his interest in geography. He is dressed like a nobleman, with his silk stockings, knee-high trousers and long jacket with a lot of buttons. The more buttons, the fancier. Wigs were powdered with flour or chalk. Some of that powder landed on his shoulders, but it was not against etiquette to show it.

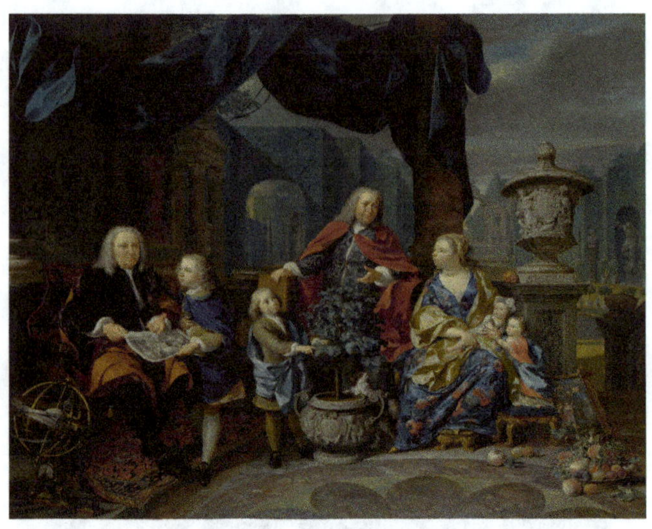

David Mollem and Jacob van Sijdervelt with his family (1740) -
Nicolaas Verkolje

Gardens were also designed in a French manner. In the family portrait by Nicolaas Verkolje we see an imaginative French garden consisting of infinite sight lines behind the triumphal arch. The bushes are well-trimmed and the garden is decorated with marble vases.

Unlike the portrait of the gentleman above by Troost, the man on the left is dressed in somber black, apparently because of his strict religious beliefs. The painting breathes an atmosphere of informality, with a casual and open body language.

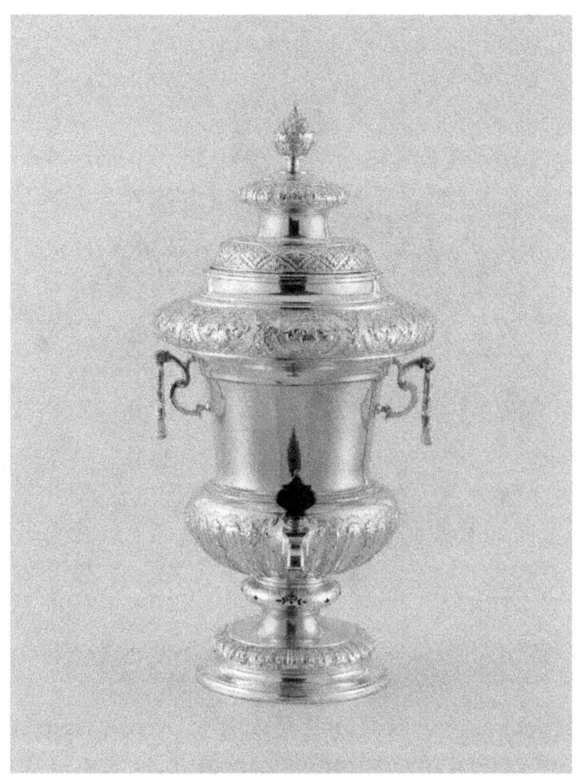

Coffee jar with tap (1729) - Andele Andeles

Coffee and tea made their way into Europe in the 18th century. To pour the coffee, one used little tanks with a tap. In Dutch, this type of object is called a *kraantjeskan*, or 'jar with tap', its design being inspired by the so-called 'wine fountains'.

The artist who made the silver coffee jar is Andele Andeles (1678 - 1754) who got his inspiration from drawings by the French engraver and architect Daniel Marot (1661 - 1752).

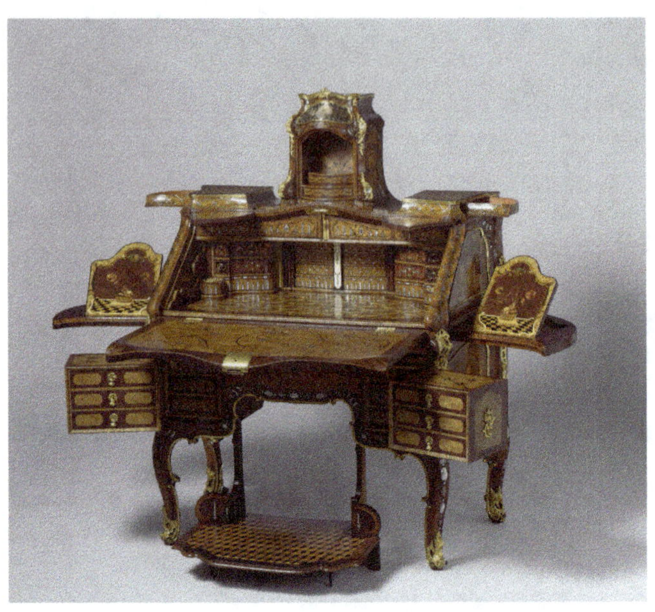

Writing desk (circa 1758 - circa 1760) - Abraham Roentgen

This desk is both a practical object and a marvel. It contains hidden drawers, openings and secret buttons to push, a specialty of Abraham Roentgen (1711 - 1795). It can even be used as a praying stool. One could kneel on the footrest. The inlay decoration looks like a three dimensional jigsaw puzzle - which it actually is. This has been achieved by a clever technique. The different inlay materials, like wood, tin or turtle shell, are glued on top of each other, with paper sheets between the layers (think of an expensive artistic lasagna). The design for the decoration is drawn on the top layer of the glued materials. The last step is to saw out the design, all layers at once, so you get multiple jig saw puzzles in exactly the same pattern. The little parts are now taken apart and glued onto the table, each part of the material of your liking.

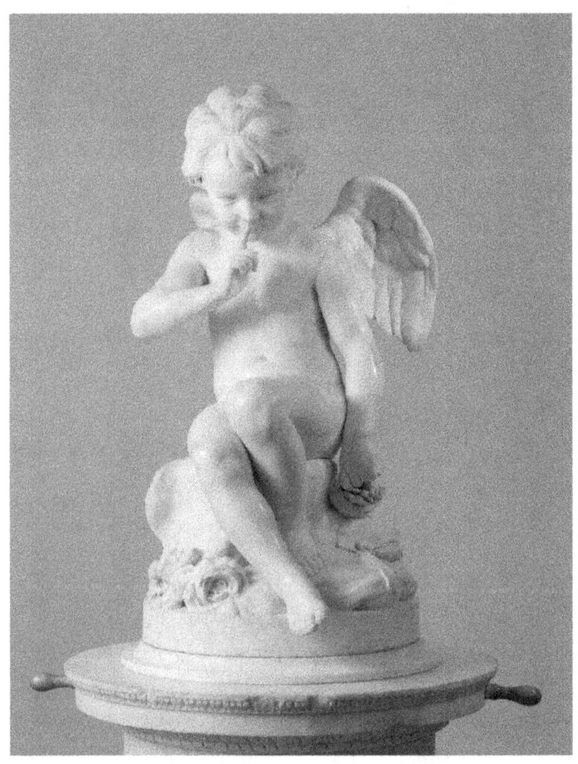

Amor (1757) - Etienne Maurice Falconet

Madame de Pompadour, mistress of King Louis XV, ordered this sculpture of 'Cupid as a menacing love' from Etienne Maurice Falconet (1716 - 1791). A quote by Voltaire is written below the smiling cherub: 'Whoever you are, this is or should be your master'.

Seated on a cloud, putting his finger on his lips, he takes an arrow out of the quiver behind him. Someone is going to fall in love soon and we are his accomplice. It is sometimes believed that the fingertip is also a symbol of hiding an affair. Look at his lifelike wings. It seems likely that Falconet examined real bird wings.

19TH-CENTURY ART

In the Netherlands the 19th century officially starts a little too early..! In 1795, inspired by the French Revolution the Dutch sack their regents and noble families to form their own democratic 'Batavian Republic'. It is the official end of the previous Republic that was so proudly established in the 17th century. What follows is a century (plus five years) of political upheaval and revolutions.

The revolution of 1795 is militarily supported by France. The Netherlands become a puppet state of the French Republic. In 1806 the country officially becomes a Kingdom under the rule of the French. This rule ends in 1813, when Napoleon is defeated and sent to the island of Elba. The independent Netherlands form a united Kingdom together with Belgium and Luxemburg. After the battle of Waterloo in 1815, Napoleon's power is over. Belgium and Luxemburg leave the Dutch Kingdom in 1839 and 1890. What remains at the end of the century is the country 'the Netherlands' as we now know it.

The swift power changes and constantly renewing political insights inspire painters and artisans. Artists like Jan Willem Pieneman and Joseph Paelinck portray the rulers of the French period. Art is heavily supported by the powerful. In the second half of the century, Socialism and Realism will influence painters and writers. Everyday people will catch their attention.

The 19th century is the era in which the Dutch discover and reinvent their own history and identity. This is the spirit of the age: all over Europe nation states form themselves, each with their own ethnography, art and national history. In art, it means that the past is shamelessly glorified and ancient styles are copied and embellished: the so-called 'neo styles'.

Rembrandt is given a status of divinity, alongside a huge statue in the center of Amsterdam. To round it off, in 1885 the Dutch construct the largest building ever made in the country, designed to house the national collection of artworks and historic objects: the 'National Museum of History and Art' also known as the Rijksmuseum.

Besides the glorification of the past there is a bustling breakthrough to the modern era. The end of the century will see the development towards modern art by the only Dutch painter that will equal Rembrandt in fame and influence: the self-taught Vincent van Gogh. Also on display in this section of the museum are artworks from the colonies under Dutch rule in the 19th century.

The depiction of the battle of Waterloo is the largest painting in the Rijksmuseum. It shows the crucial moment in the fight that brought down Napoleon. The Duke of Wellington in the middle, seated on his horse, hears of the arrival of his Prussian allies. He points in the direction of the French army as a signal to charge. On a stretcher on the left we see the wounded prince Willem Frederik of Orange who would later become King Willem II of the Netherlands. He looks confident and relaxed, knowing that victory is near. Later he would become known as the 'Hero of Waterloo'. Less fortunate is the English colonel De Lancey, seen in the front right. He would die a few minutes after hearing the good news.

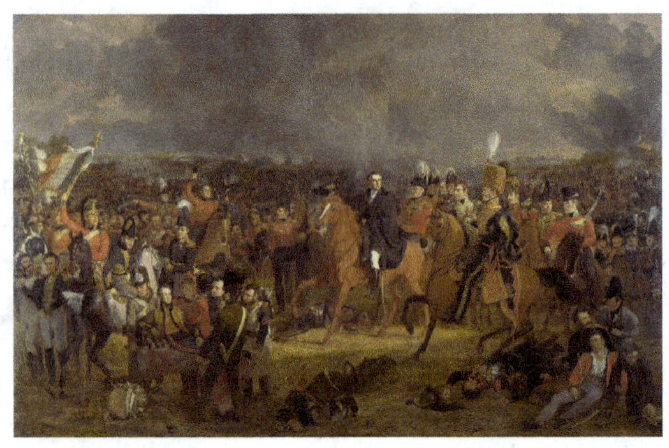

The Battle of Waterloo (1824) - Jan Willem Pieneman

On the far left we see the French general Cambronne, the loser of the battle. Almost invisible next to the tower in the background is Napoleon. He can be identified by his cocked hat and white horse. The painter Jan Willem Pieneman (1779 - 1853) aimed not only to show victors and losers but also the grim atmosphere of the battlefield. Grey clouds hang over the landscape densely packed with people.

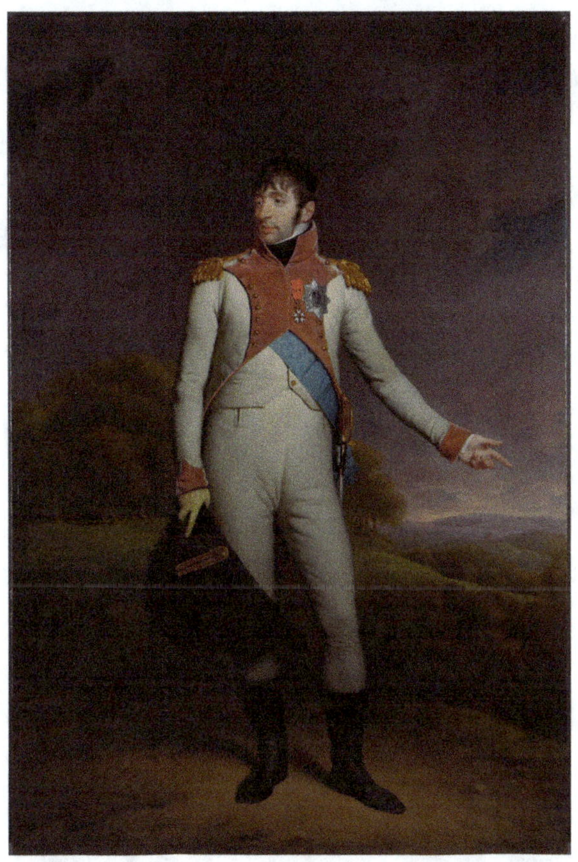

Portrait of Louis Napoleon (1809) - Charles Howard Hodges

The first King of the Netherlands was not Dutch, but French. Louis Napoleon, a brother of Napoleon Bonaparte was appointed 'King of Holland' in 1806, when the country was taken by the French. In spite of being the representative of an occupying power, he was named 'the good King'. He supported the arts and reformed tax laws and civil laws. In cases of disaster, such as explosions in factories or floods, he was present to help and give money to those stricken. He made Amsterdam the capital of the country and turned the Town Hall on Dam Square into his palace.

He also tried to speak Dutch, which resulted in a famous speech where he called himself 'King of Holland' ('Koning van Holland). His French accent made 'King' (ko*ning*) sound like 'rabbit' (ko*nijn*), but he was forgiven for this mistake. It only added to his popularity.

61

In the painting by Hodges (1764 - 1837) Louis shows he is a normal man in spite of his status. He is not portrayed in a castle wearing luxurious clothes but outdoors wearing a colonel's costume. His left hand used to hold a staff but that has been retouched. Looking closely you can still see the traces on the canvas. Also note the scar under his left eye, a souvenir from the many battles he fought for his brother. Louis Napoleon had the national art collection in The Hague moved to his palace in Amsterdam. This collection formed the core of what later became the Rijksmuseum.

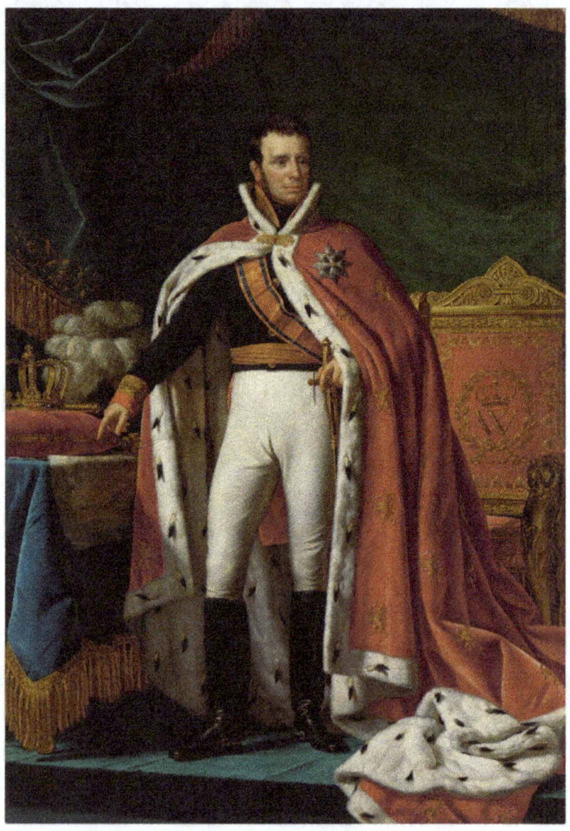

Portrait of King Willem I (1819) - Joseph Paelinck

After the first defeat of Napoleon in 1813, the 'United States of the Netherlands' were formed, a Kingdom consisting of the Netherlands, Luxemburg and Belgium. The first King of this country is shown here: Willem I. He also ruled over the colonies of the Dutch: the East Indies, the

Dutch Antilles and Surinam. In this portrait he points at a map showing the East Indies with its capital Batavia, now Jakarta. He is dressed in an ermine cloak, with his crown on the table. This is the leader of an empire.

Willem I was the 'Merchant King'. He founded the Dutch Bank and the Dutch-East India Trading Company. During his reign, canals, roads and bridges were built. The colonies were forced to export 20 percent of what they produced to the Netherlands, which stimulated the Dutch economy.

Willem I also believed that art was an important factor in society. Not only did he enlarge the art collection already formed by Louis Napoleon, he also founded institutions for art education, the Royal Academies. He installed two museums, one in The Hague, now known as the *Mauritshuis*, and one in Amsterdam, the current *Rijksmuseum*. He bought 300 more paintings during his reign.

In spite of his efforts to build a new country, Willem I was unsuccessful in keeping his country unified. In 1839, the southern provinces split from the Kingdom to form Belgium.

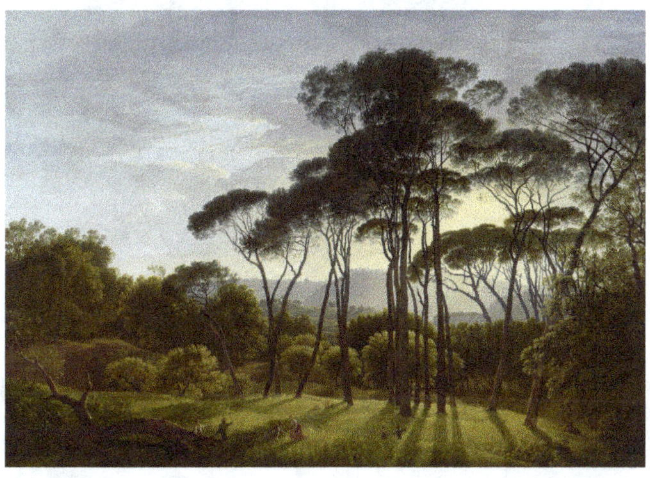

Italian landscape with pines (1807) - Hendrik Voogd

This painting is not a Dutch landscape, but an Italian landscape painted by a Dutch artist, Hendrik Voogd (1768 - 1839). In 1788, he received an endowment to study art in Rome.

During his stay in Rome he became part of a group of landscape painters who were particularly interested in light effects. This painting shows his magnificent technique. The brushstrokes are nearly invisible, the light is cool but radiant and the trees are represented in microscopic detail. Voogd spent the rest of his life in Italy, but he is still considered a Dutch painter.

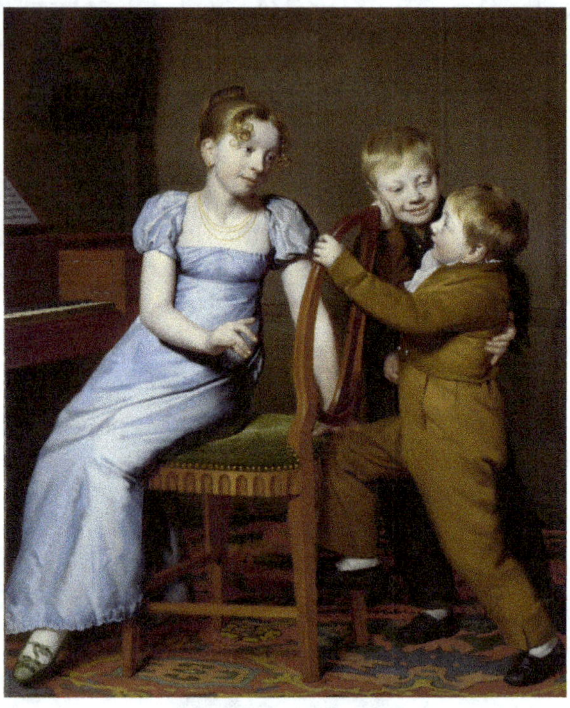

Piano playing disturbed (1813) - Willem Bartel van der Kooi

A girl in a blue dress tries to play the piano but is disturbed by her younger brother. This scene depicted by Willem Bartel van der Kooi (1768 - 1836) looks informal but is very well composed. The children form a triangle in the middle of the composition. The folds and shadows in the girl's dress are meticulously painted. The softness of the cushion on the chair and the fabric of the children's clothes is almost tangible. Their faces are lively and realistic.

High society will do everything to show its wealth in portraits. The painter Jan Adam Kruseman (1804 - 1862) was very popular as a portraitist of the well-to-do.

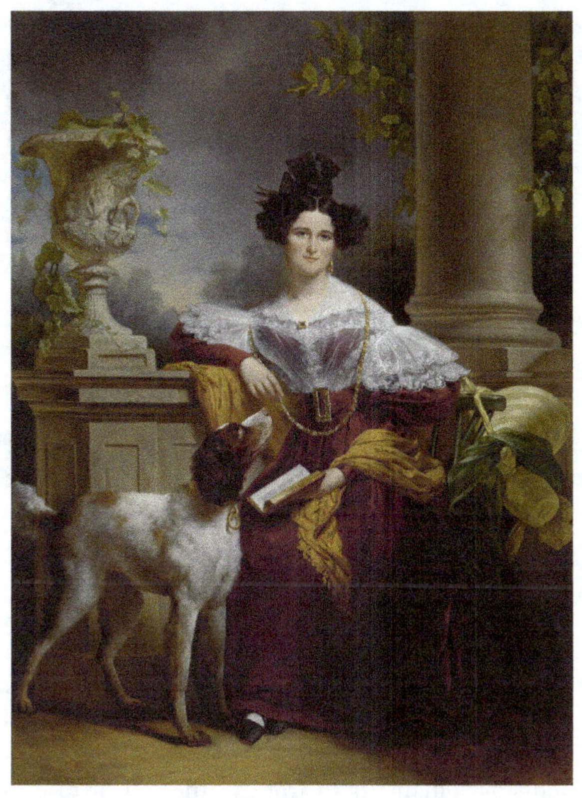

Portrait of Alida Christina Assink (1833) - Jan Adam Kruseman

The lady portrayed here is the 23-year old Alida Christina Assink. Her hoop dress has puffed sleeves and she wears a 'canezou', a kind of transparent jacket. A belt with a big buckle suggests a slim waist.

To give the portrait some international allure, elements from English portraiture have been added: the hunting-dog, the marble vase and the column to her right. The setting is pastoral and dreamy.

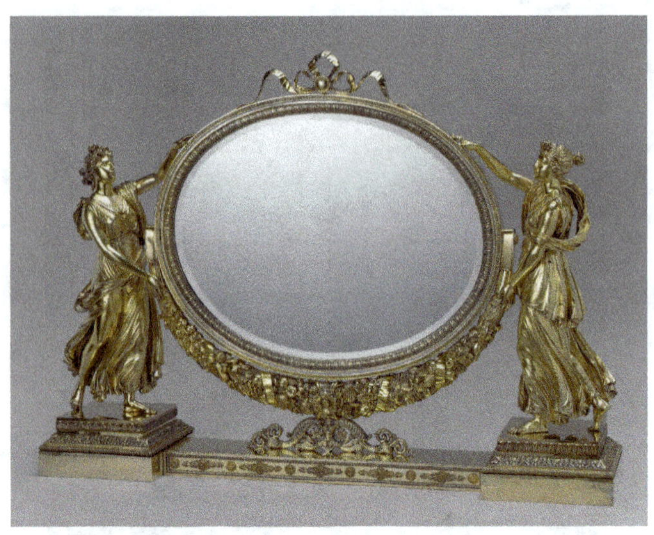

Mirror (1828-1829) - Joseph-Germain Dutalis and Louis Royer

This mirror is an example of the 'Empire' style. Elegant, symmetric and decorated with classical elements like flowers and swans. Two nymphs hold the mirror upright. One of them has flowers in her hair, which symbolizes 'day'. The other has her hair tied up as a symbol of 'night'. They represent the two moments a woman sits in front of the mirror to do her hair and make-up, the morning and the evening. The clothes of the nymphs flap as if moved by wind.

The mirror of gilded silver was part of a set of toiletries, a gift from King Willem I for his daughter Marianne who was to marry Prince Albert of Prussia. By giving such an exquisite object the King could show the rest of Europe his wealth and ambition. Only really powerful men could afford such a present. Funnily enough, objects like these were not in use for a long time but exhibited as art works after a few years.

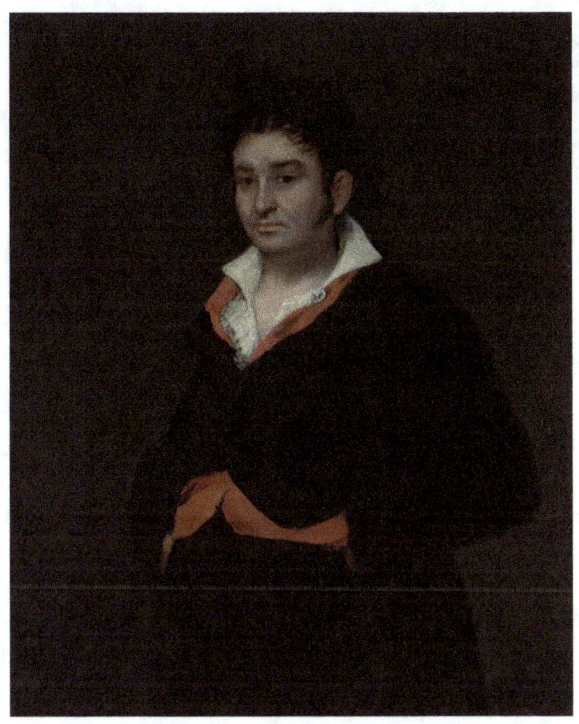

Portrait of Don Ramó Satué (1823) - Francisco Goya

Don Ramón Satué was a Spanish judge who fiercely opposed the occupation of Spain by the troops of Napoleon. After the French occupation he was appointed judge at the Supreme Court of Spain.

Although he is a man with a high public position, in this painting he is informal, pensive and not at all impeccably dressed. He even has his hands in his pockets. The combination of a dark suit against a neutral background makes way for one beautiful accent in the composition, the red of his vest.

The Spanish painter Francisco de Goya y Lucientes (1746 - 1828) is known for his portraits of members of the Spanish Court and his surrealistic drawings. Because of the informal posture and the open shirt of his model this painting is believed to be a friendship portrait.

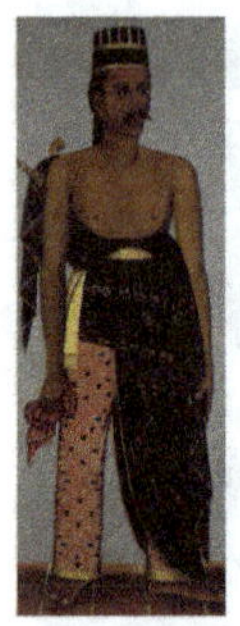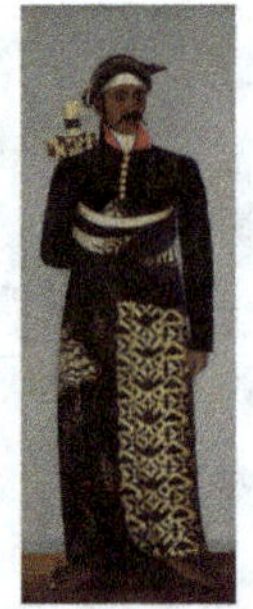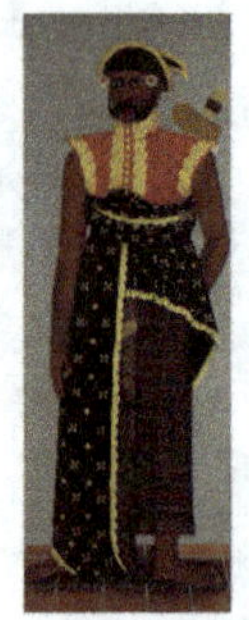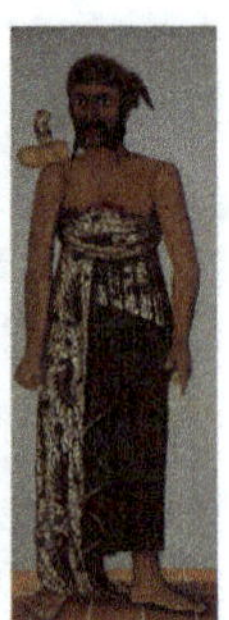

Court officials from Java, by anonymous artist, circa 1820-1870

The Dutch East Indies, nowadays known as Indonesia, were a Dutch colony until 1949, and one of the most profitable parts of the Kingdom with a perfect climate to grow spices. The Dutch and East Indian cultures had a big influence on each other. In these four paintings, out of a series of five, we see prototypes of court officials from Java. It is believed that the painter was not a Western artist. The descent, rank and status of these Javanese court officials is shown by their garments with batik motifs and their weapons.

The third man wears a jacket in western style. It is very rare to see Javanese portrayed like this. Normally, the Dutch would depict them as servile subjects, dangerous opponents or unspoiled savages.

The man on the far right is a body guard. His clothes show the wings of a 'garuda', half man, half eagle. His garment is somewhat shorter, so he can spring to action if needed.

The second man is a 'mantri', an administrator. His garments shows feathers of chickens and peacocks. The black band around the hilt of his sword ('kris') shows his high status.

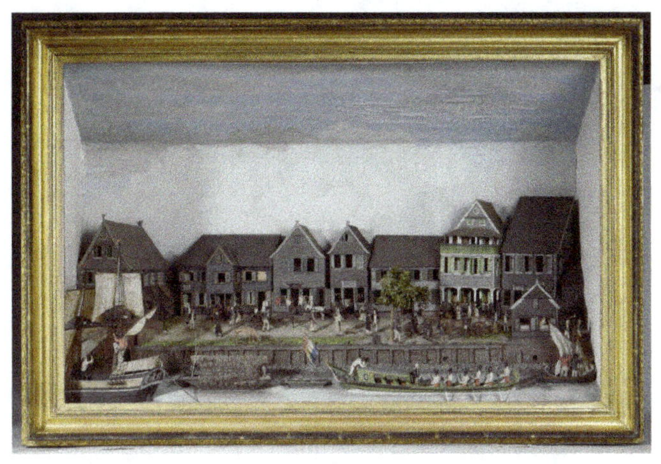

Diorama of the waterfront in Paramaribo (1820) - Gerrit Schouten

Suriname was a Dutch colony until 1975. It was traded with the English for the island of Manhattan in 1667. Because of the fertile soil in this country the Dutch started a lot of plantations and built a city, Paramaribo.

In this wooden diorama, we see a detailed depiction of a particular part of Paramaribo the waterfront. The waterfront along the Suriname River was the vital hub of Surinamese trade.

The artist Gerrit Schouten (1779 - 1839) made an exact copy of the street with its houses, including house numbers, drainpipes and different types of ships. People of various ethnic origins walk about. Take a closer look to find the vicar with his green parasol and the white merchant with his slave carrying his goods.

At the left we see a merchantman sailing out. The boat next to it carries goods to the plantations. The man who commissioned the diorama, British merchant William Leckie, lived in the green house.

A year after the diorama was made, in 1821, the waterfront was completely destroyed by fire. One night, four hundred houses and 800 hundred warehouses were lost, as well as churches, a theatre and a weighing-house.

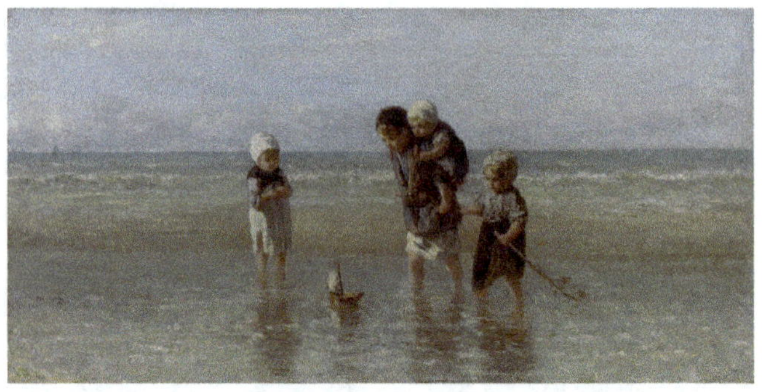

Children of the sea (1872) - Jozef Israëls

What looks like a group of children playing in the water is not a happy painting. The children are not on a day out, they are from a poor fisherman's family. They don't play and they don't smile. The elder boy carries his youngest sister, a foreboding of his future responsibilities. The paper boat will be a real fisherman's boat later. The girl on the left looks like a fisherwoman waiting for her husband to return from the dangerous sea.

Paintings by Jozef Israëls (1824 - 1891) were very popular at the time. He created his paintings in the style of the Hague School representing ordinary farmers and fishermen, depicted in broad brushstrokes.

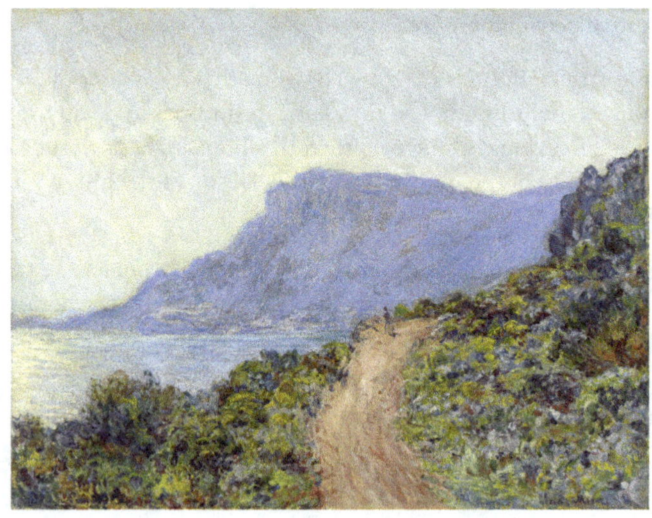

La Corniche near Monaco (1884) - Claude Monet

Impressionist painters worked with swift and loose brushstrokes to catch the first impression of an object or a landscape. Claude Monet (1840 - 1926) is one of the founding fathers of this new style. He had an important influence on Dutch painters such as Breitner and Willem Witsen. The painting is one of Monet's first works ever to be shown in public in the Netherlands. The warmth and dreamy character are unmistakably his.

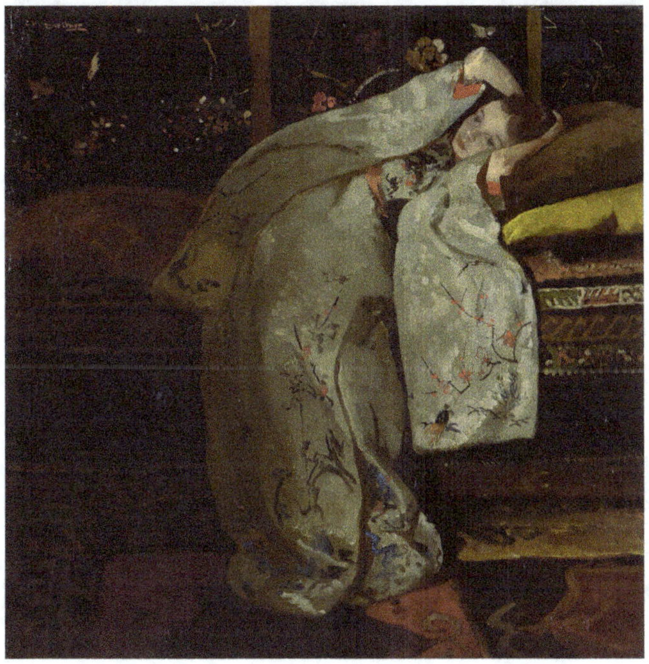

Girl in a white Kimono (1894) - Georg Hendrik Breitner

The painter George Hendrik Breitner (1857 - 1923), made a series of twelve paintings of a girl in a kimono around the year 1894, only one of which is in the Rijksmuseum. Like many artists at the end of the 19th century, Breitner was inspired by Japanese art. Not only the outfit of the girl is Japanese, but also the folding screen in the back and the decoration of the cushions.

From a technical point of view this is also a Japanese painting. Not so much the person in the painting is important, but the composition that consists of flat surfaces and clear colors. The cushions, kimono and background form a unity.

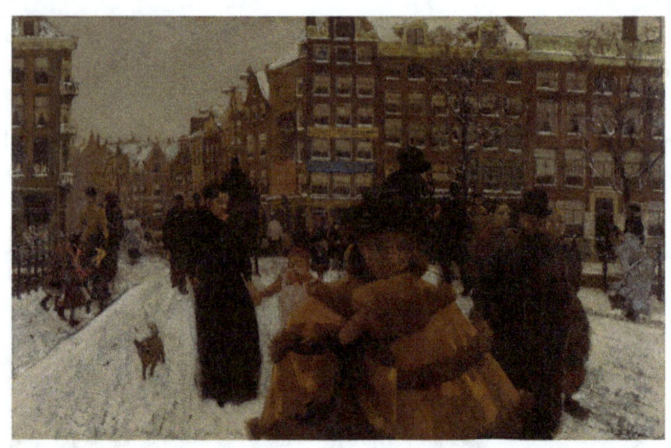

Bridge over Singel, near Paleisstraat (1896) - George Hendrik Breitner

In this painting we see people crossing a bridge in Amsterdam near Dam Square. A well-dressed lady in the middle walks right towards us. For a lot of his paintings, George Breitner made photos as a preparation. This was criticized by traditional art lovers, but Breitner simply stated that with this mechanical aid he could focus better on details while painting.

The composition, however, is very much like a photo: very direct, sharply cut and almost like a snapshot. The paint has been applied to the canvas with a light touch.

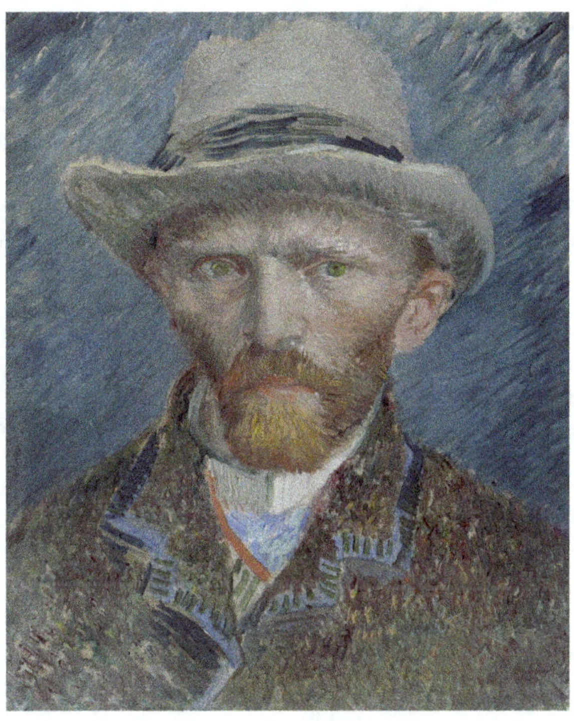

This is one of the many self-portraits Van Gogh produced. It shows the style which made him famous: the expressive brush strokes and the daring color combinations. Even though Van Gogh worked quickly, he always knew exactly what he was doing.

The different elements like the background, the jacket and the face are painted in different 'rhythms': there is a variation of long and short strokes of the brush next to broad and small stripes, dots and lines. His eyes are of a fiery green, his ginger beard a mixture of many color tones.

Together with Rembrandt, Vincent van Gogh (1853 - 1890) is the most famous painter of the Netherlands. After pursuing different careers as an art merchant and a pastor, Van Gogh decided to devote his life entirely to painting at the age of twenty-seven. He lived and worked in the Netherlands, England, Belgium and France. As an artist, he was almost entirely self-taught, seeking inspiration from old masters and colleagues.

Van Gogh loved to read about art and was an avid museum goer. In 1885 he paid a visit to the Rijksmuseum, where he spent hours in front of *The*

Jewish Bride. In letters to his friends and family he wrote about his love for this work by Rembrandt:

> 'Could you believe that I would give ten years of my life to spend two weeks alone with this painting?'

The Rijksmuseum only has this one self-portrait by Vincent van Gogh in its collection.

For more information on his life and works, please see the Van Gogh Museum guide in this series. The Van Gogh museum is the world's authority on Van Gogh and is just a two-minute walk from the Rijksmuseum.

20TH-CENTURY ART

Although most people know the Rijksmuseum as the museum with *The Night Watch* its task is much bigger than just preserving this world famous masterwork. The official title of the museum is 'National Museum of History and Art'. The Rijksmuseum keeps track of current developments and shows contemporary objects alongside the Dutch Masters. The museum has an impressive collection of modern art on the top floors. Objects range from paintings and photographs to models, furniture and typographic designs.

Due to copyright restrictions it is unfortunately not possible to show the most recent acquisitions. In addition, many art works of the 20th century are on loan from other museums. Therefore, this chapter is limited compared to the rest of this guide.

Since the Rijksmuseum is also guardian of Dutch history, objects like planes and guns are very common to find in this museum, especially if they are also interesting from a designer's point of view. The biplane 'Bantam' was built in 1917. (It cannot be reproduced here due to copyright issues). Its purpose was to fight on the British side during World War I. The designer is the Dutch engineer Frits Koolhoven (1886 - 1946), who worked for the British Aerial Transport Company. The 'Bantam' is a one-seat plane made of wood and was tested with different engines, making a huge impression at various aerial shows

The 19th and 20th century are the ages of the technical revolutions, in a world that was still steeped in age-old political relations.

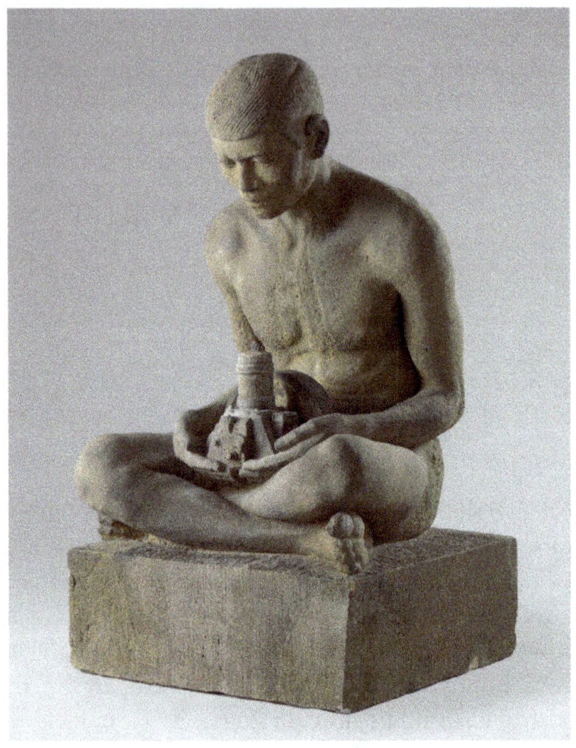

Man and Machine (circa 1913) - Marinus Johannes Hack

This statue made by J.M. Hack (1871 - 1939) shows a man from the Dutch East Indies, nowadays known as Indonesia. It was made as decoration for a firm producing machinery for colonial companies. The man is portrayed as a native working with his hands. The machine he holds symbolizes the idea of the good influence of Dutch technical standards and welfare on the lives of the original inhabitants of the Indies.

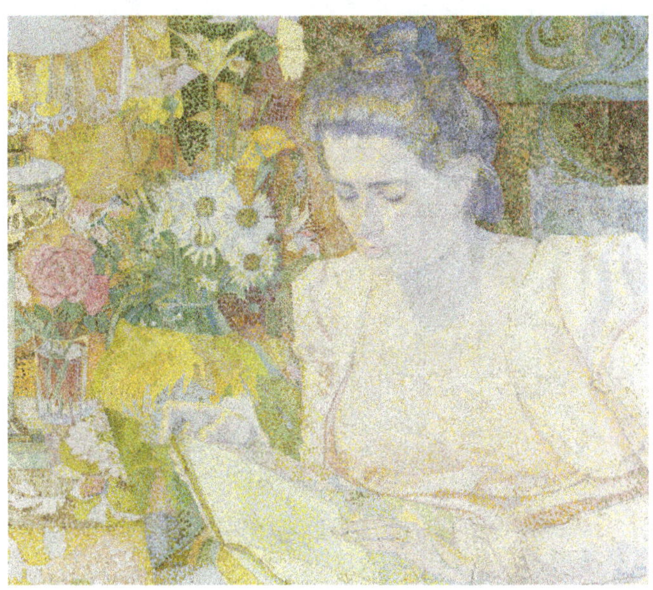

Portrait of Marie Jeannette de Lange (1900) - Jan Toorop

The lady reading in this colorful painting is the chairwoman of the 'Association for the Improvement of Women's Clothing', Marie Jeanette de Lange. She is portrayed in the clothes she promoted, loose-fitting and comfortable.

The painter Jan Toorop (1858 - 1928) made this portrait in a pointillist style. The picture is a true feast of colors, and never ceases to amaze. Its colors are light and vibrant, the brushstrokes are mere dots and dashes.

ASIAN ART

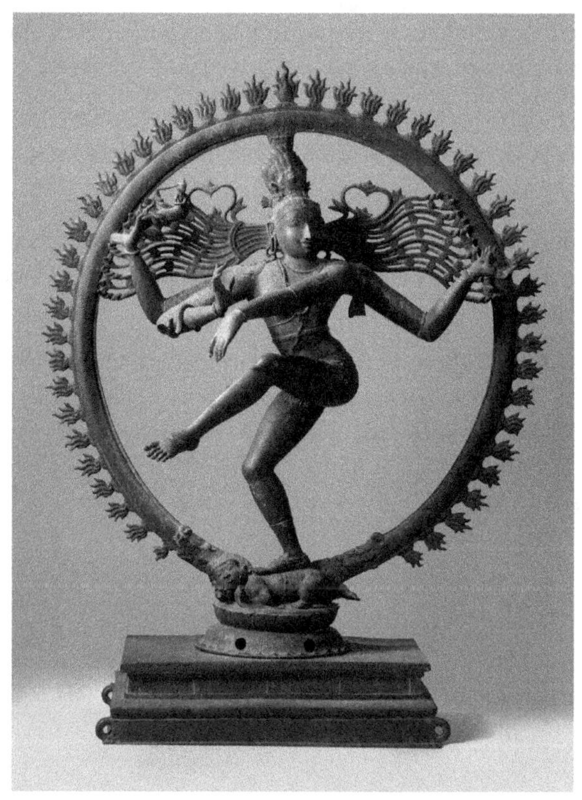

Shiva Nataraja (12th century), India, Tamil Nadu

The Rijksmuseum has an exquisite collection of Asian art. To house this collection, a special pavilion was built in the garden. From the outside this pavilion looks like a closed structure, but inside it is open space, tranquil and light.

Floating like a flower in a pond of the Rijksmuseum garden, this section is one of the gems. This part of the collection does not have a storyline or central theme. Top works are shown from different countries and periods.

The god Shiva is both creator and destroyer of the world. In this bronze statue he is shown in his incarnation as Nataraja, the king of dance. Creation is symbolized by the drum in his right back hand. Vibrations are new life. Purifying destruction is shown by the fire in his left back hand. By the combination of these elements, Shiva shows perfect balance. He dances in a controlled way and superior posture, surrounded by a circle of cosmic fire, while his right foot crushes a dwarf, symbol of ignorance.

On feast days, richly decorated bronze figures of Hindu gods were carried in procession. Carrying poles would be inserted through the rings on the base.

For Shiva's followers, watching the god dance is a blessing that gives deeper insights that can lead to salvation. He is the symbol of constant change, the universe in movement.

Religious objects like these have more than just artistic value. They form a link between heaven and earth. Therefore, works like these were manufactured according to strict protocol. In Western societies, saints and relics played a similar role, being mediators between the human and divine worlds. For every aspect of daily life, there is a deity you can address.

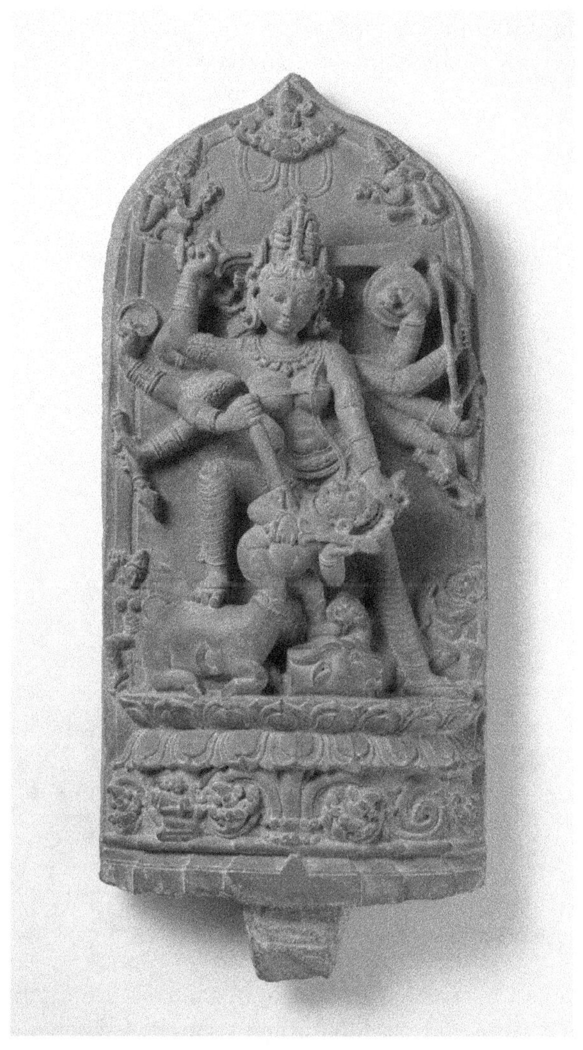

Durga killing the Buffalo demon (circa 1000-circa 1100 A.D.)
Bangladesh

The goddess Durga kills the demon Mahisha in a magnificent display of movement and force. In her ten hands she holds various weapons. She stabs the demon that comes out of a decapitated bull. If you look closely, you will notice that the lion at her feet helps her fight.

The whole scene is set on a lotus flower. This flower grows out of mud through troubled water towards the sunlight and is therefore a symbol of enlightenment. Demons and gods are in constant battle in Hinduism. The evil demons destroy balance, after which the gods have to restore it again.

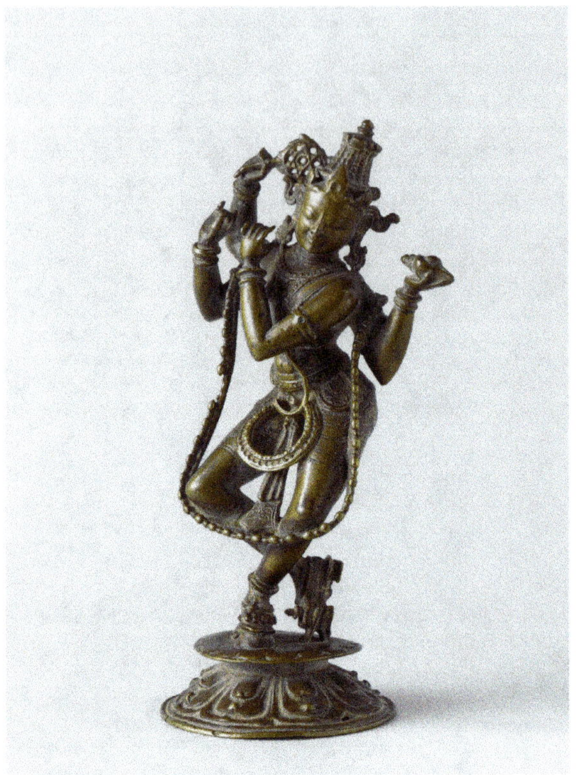

Krishna playing the flute (circa 1500-circa 1700), India, Orissa

Krishna is one of the ten appearances or *avatars* of Vishnu, the guardian of cosmic balance. Born and raised a farmer's son, he is known for his beauty and his flute playing. In this brass sculpture he is shown dancing and playing, with garlands of flowers hanging from his shoulders. The chakra and shell in his back hands identify him as Krishna. With his beauty and talent, he lures women to leave their sleeping husbands at night and dance with him in the forest. He is therefore known as the symbol of total surrender to god and of unification with him. Like Durga above, the foot of this sculpture is a lotus flower, the symbol of enlightenment.

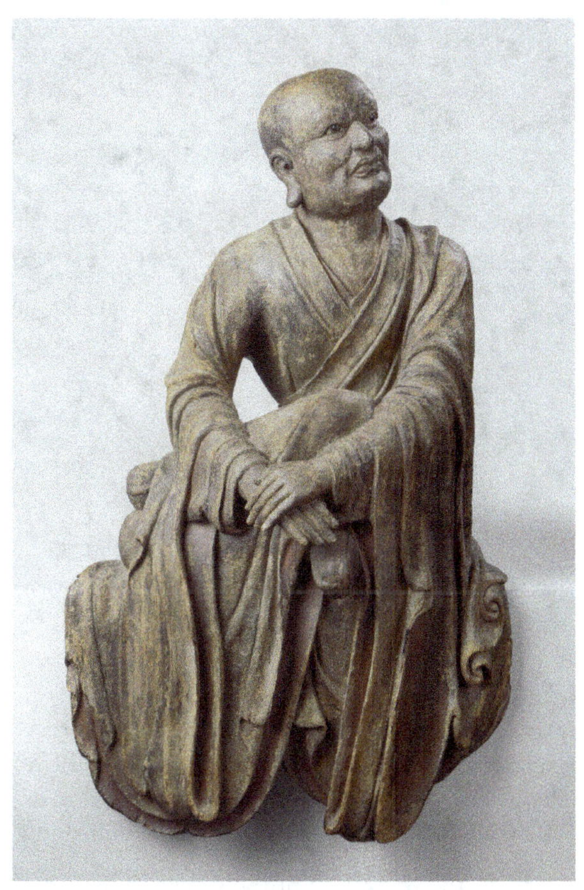

A lohan (circa 1200-circa 1400), China

A lohan is a follower of Buddha who has accomplished spiritual perfection. He guards the Buddhist law until the Buddha himself returns to earth. A lohan lives as a hermit in the mountains and has supernatural powers. His big earlobes, symbols of knowledge, identify him as a monk. Although he sits comfortably, his torso and face are turned upwards because he listens intently to the recitation of a 'sutra', a text of the Buddhist law. The eyes in this wooden sculpture are made of glass which makes them shimmer and emphasize his intelligence.

In the Asian pavilion of the Rijksmuseum this lohan is located in front of the stairs leading to the ground floor. You cannot miss him while visiting the pavilion. He will look right at you.

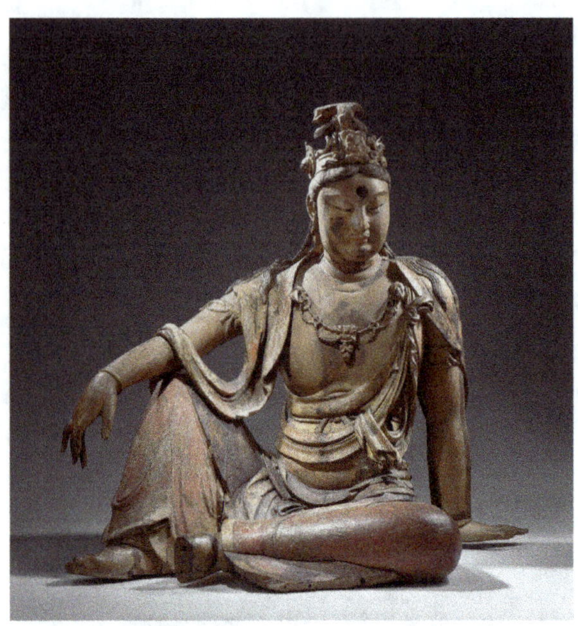

Guanyin (circa 1100-circa 1200 A.D.), China

The Buddhist deity Guanyin is a savior of people in distress. According to legend he was once found in this posture, meditating on the reflection of the moonlight in the water. That is why the god is looking down. The moon on the surface of the water is a symbol of transience and illusion.

His pose is known as 'the relaxation of the Great King', with his left leg on the floor and his right leg supporting his arm. Under his tiara his braids hang loosely on his shoulders. His whole demeanor radiates tranquillity and concentration.

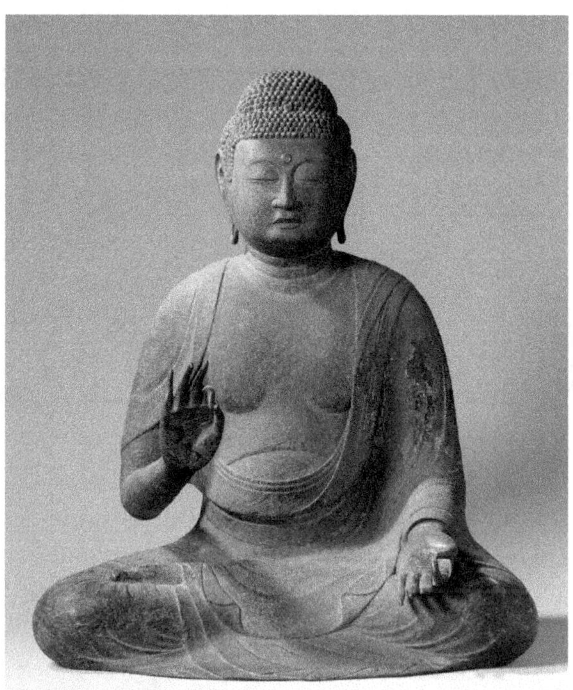

Buddha Amida (circa 1125-circa 1175), Japan

The Buddha Amida is a Buddha for simple believers. No complex rituals are needed to show you the way to the Truth. Simply but sincerely believing in Amida and invoking him will open the gates of Paradise. It is a direct and emotional connection to the Buddha. In this sculpture we recognize him by the three wrinkles around his neck, the big earlobes and the bulge on his head. He holds his right hand, with membranes between the fingers, in the teaching position. Thumb and index finger touch each other at the tips.

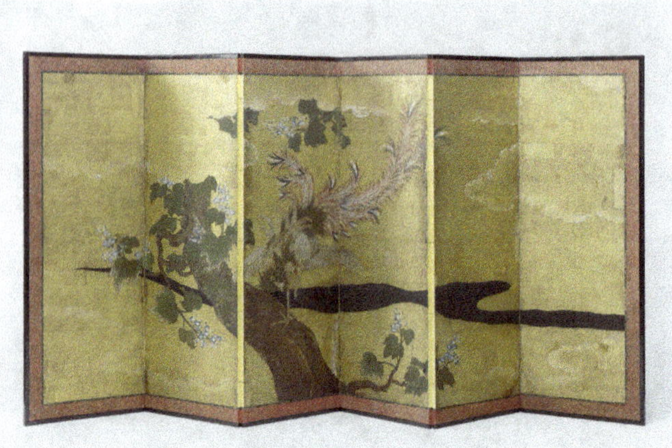

This folding screen forms an ensemble with a second screen. Like in Japanese scripture we have to read from right to left. The screens symbolize the transition from winter to spring. Folding screens were only used during the season which they represent.

A mythological hoo bird is depicted on the left screen. Together with the paulownia tree it is a symbol of sound statesmanship, and a popular subject for works of art of the ruling Japanese elite in the Edo period (1600-1868).

At that time Japan was largely cut off from the world; the ships depicted in the right screen come from two of the very few countries that had access to Japan, namely China and the Netherlands.

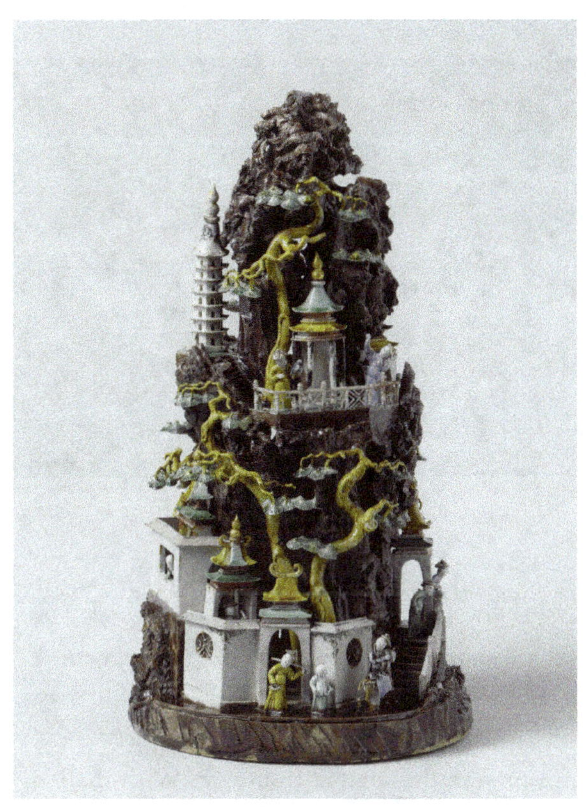

Miniature Garden (circa 1700-circa 1724)

Gardens can even be found inside the Rijksmuseum..! This beautiful porcelain rock with garden is one of the 'must sees' of the Asian collection. The object seems to have been made at the beginning of the 18th century, during the late Kangxi-period (1662 - 1722).

A rock is shown with a pathway leading to the top. Alongside the path there are garden houses and trees. Were this real, everywhere you would walk you could take a seat to enjoy the scenery. The rock has been put together like a jigsaw puzzle. The refinement in details is breathtaking. Take a close look at the people strolling about, the trees and the pagodas. It is almost like reading a storybook. The garden represents the universe.

This miniature rock was perhaps a table decoration of a so-called 'literate'. Literates were administrators who were confined to a life of writing and copying texts at their desks. This miniature universe would inspire them to work or write a poem or maybe even to paint.

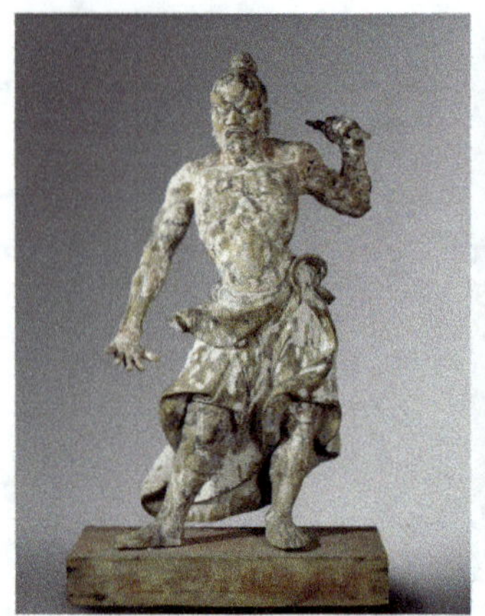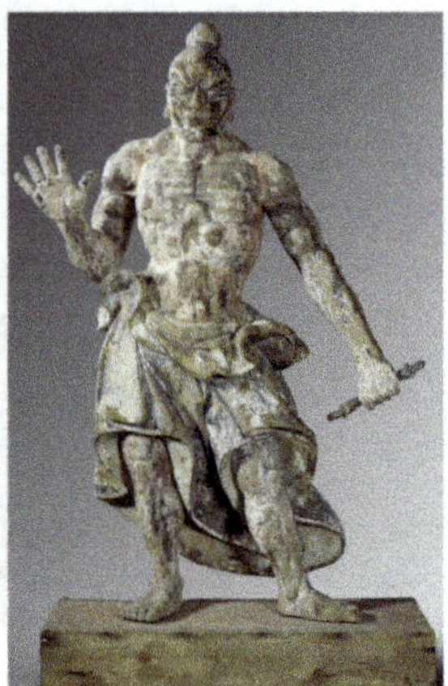

Temple guards (14th century), Japan

These impressive creatures are temple guards from Japan. Every Buddhist temple has two figures like these at the entrance. They are big muscular men with a fierce look in their eyes.

Their task is to protect the temple from evil. With their right hand they keep off any unwanted visitors. In their left hand they keep a diamond 'vajra', with which they can crush ignorance. Notice how one of the guards has his mouth open and the other one closed. They symbolize the open beginning ('a!') and the closed end ('un!') of their Siddham alphabet. All other sounds and writings, in fact all knowledge, lies between those two sounds. He who enters the temple will acquire this knowledge. The statues are made of wood.

We can still see the traces of the paint of their original decoration. Take a look inside them, you will see the original beams on which the statues were placed. Although the men look quite impressive, they are mild-tempered and stand for all good in the world.

In Japanese culture they are well-loved. On special holidays, children crawl between their legs to gain a bit of their power. To plea for the sick and weak, people attach written messages to the temple gate protected by these guards.

SPECIAL COLLECTIONS

The Special Collections section is the 'surprise act' of the Rijksmuseum. Unlike the top floors, where the art works are arranged according to century, the Special Collections galleries are like a big candy box of art with small-scale exhibitions in every room. Each room is a treat, and the way the objects are displayed is superb.

You will find ships' models, porcelain tea sets, engraved glass and silver, but also magic lanterns that still work, a silent disco in the music section and much, much more. You will feel like a child in a toy store.

A few highlights of the Special Collection are shown below.

The Rijksmuseum has a large collection of slides that were used with the magic lantern. Just like nowadays watching a Netflix episode together, people would visit each other to look at the slides and tell each other the stories that go with them. Not only was this is a serious pastime with educational purposes, there was also room for fun. Scary faces, midgets and weird animals were shown.

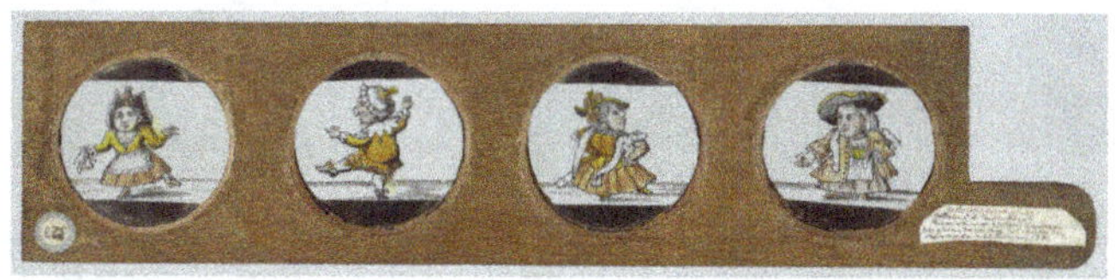

Four midgets, by anonymous artist (circa 1710-circa 1790

The Netherlands have a long and impressive maritime history. The world power of the 17th century was partly founded on a worldwide network of colonies and coast fortifications. By 1650, the Dutch had the largest fleet in the world and Amsterdam was known to have the world's biggest harbor. The old trade of building wooden ships is still preserved in the ships models section.

Besides models of complete ships you will find compasses, canons and ships decorations. This model of a 19th- century submarine is on display as well.

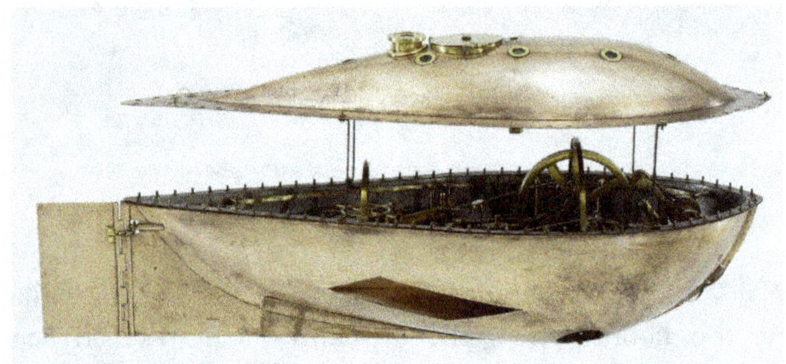

Model of a submarine (1835-1840) - Antoine Lipkens

LOCATION AND TICKETS

For up-to-date information on opening hours, ticket prices and directions, please visit the Rijksmuseum website:

www.rijksmuseum.nl

The Rijksmuseum is located at Museumplein, the cultural heart of Amsterdam where you will find three internationally renowned museums and one of the most beautiful concert halls in the world, the Concertgebouw, all within a 3-minute walking range.

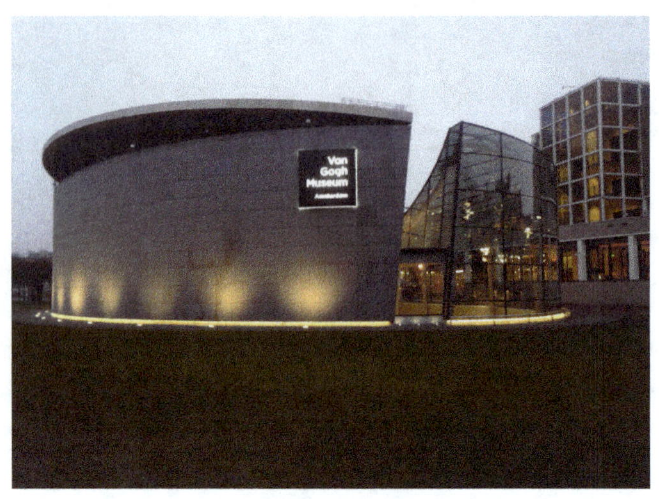

The Van Gogh Museum has the world's largest collection of Van Gogh's paintings and drawings. Photo Amsterdam Publishers.

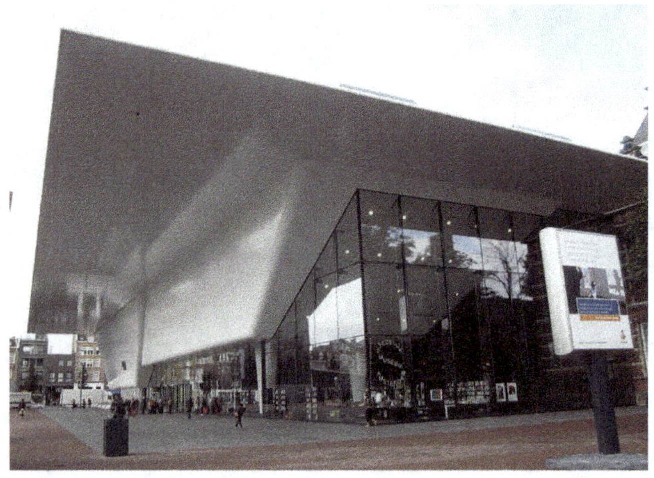

The Stedelijk Museum is the most important museum in the Netherlands for modern and contemporary art. Copyright Creative Commons.

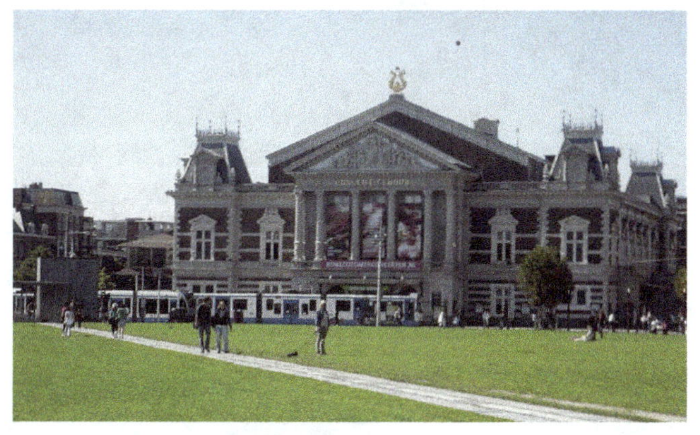

The Concertgebouw, from Museumplein. It has the world's finest acoustics for classical music. Copyright Creative Commons, Supercarwaar.

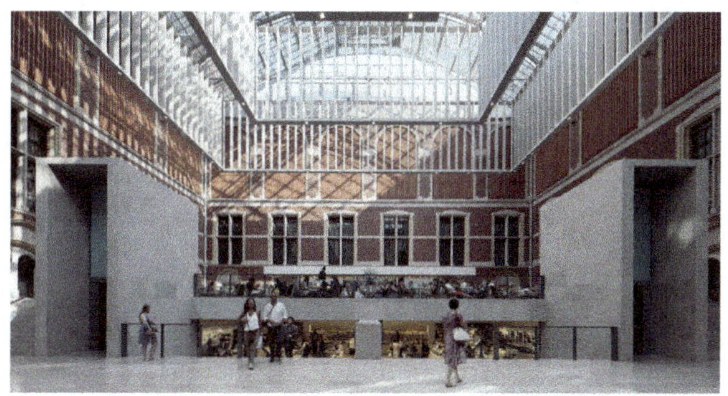

Atrium of the Rijksmuseum. Architect: Cruz y Ortiz. Picture by Wikimedia Commons.

ANNE FRANK HOUSE

ANNE'S SECRET ANNEX TURNED INTO MUSEUM

MARKO KASSENAAR

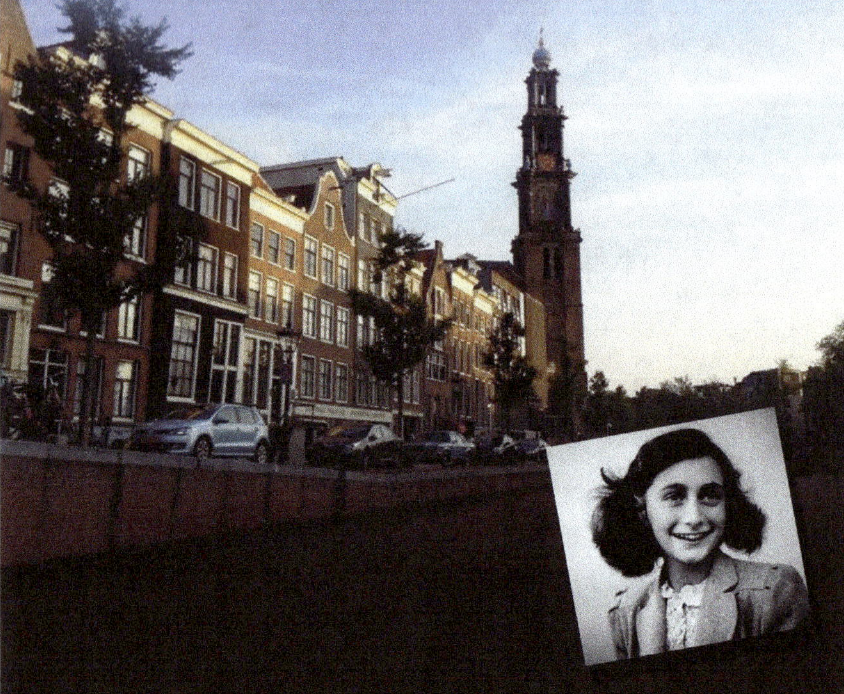

ANNE FRANK
HOUSE
AMSTERDAM

INTRODUCTION

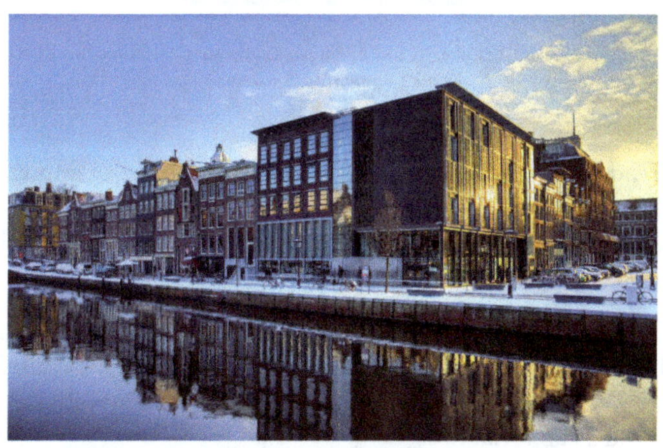

The Anne Frank House on an early winter morning - photo by
Dennis van de Water

The Anne Frank House is the most famous museum in Amsterdam and attracts over a million visitors a year. A visit to the Anne Frank House, the house on Prinsengracht in Amsterdam where Anne and her family went into hiding during the Second World War, will undoubtedly have a profound emotional impact on you. The story of a young Jewish girl growing up under dangerous circumstances and writing down her innermost feelings is touching. Anne Frank has rightly become the symbol of the Holocaust.

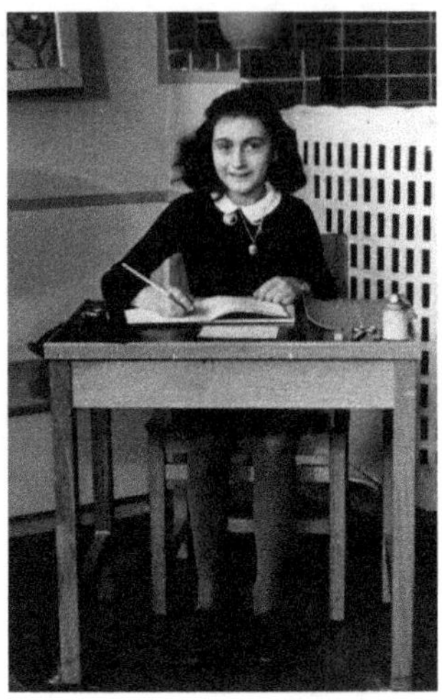

Anne Frank (1940), By unknown photographer, Collection Anne Frank Foundation Amsterdam

You will read about Anne Frank and her family, the secret annex, the daily life in the annex, the betrayal, some facts and figures about Jews in Amsterdam, the building of the Anne Frank House, and the Anne Frank Tree.

The Anne Frank House consists of two parts. The former hiding place behind the office of Anne Frank's father is a walk-through part, refurbished in 1930s style. The modern wing houses temporary exhibitions and has a bookshop and a cafeteria.

When you visit the Anne Frank House, a special route leads you from room to room. You can visit the living room, the kitchen and Anne Frank's room, where you can see the pictures of art works, film stars and royals she stuck on her wall. Not all of the rooms are open to the public.

THE FRANK FAMILY

Anne Frank was born on 12 June 1929 in Frankfurt am Main (Germany), where her father Otto Frank was a banker. After Hitler's rise to power in 1933, the Frank family fled to the much safer Holland. Otto Frank, his wife Edith, and their two children Margot (1926) and Anne (1929) settled in Amsterdam, where they led a happy life and where Otto Frank became a spice merchant.

Their life dramatically changed in May 1940 when the Nazi's occupied the Netherlands. Gradually, the Germans denied the Jews many rights. They were, for example, no longer allowed to use public transport, they were not allowed to own a business, they had to stay inside after 8 pm. Anne and Margot had to go to an all-Jewish school. In order to keep his own business, Otto Frank had to formally change its ownership.

On 8 July 1942 the Frank family received a letter from the German occupiers calling up Margot Frank to go to a labour camp in Germany. The family did not trust the situation. To avoid deportation, they decided to carry out the plan they had been preparing for months, and moved to live secretly behind Otto Frank's company office on Prinsengracht. This hiding place was suggested to Otto Frank by his business partner Johannes Kleinmann.

Four employees, Miep Gies, Bep Voskuijl, Johannes Kleinmann and Victor Kugler, were informed that the Frank family were going to live in the annex behind the office, and all agreed to help, despite the fact that punishments were severe for helping out Jews. They did not hesitate to take on the responsibility of this risky task.

Before going into hiding they stocked up some hundred tins of food and other household products. Victor Kugler came up with the brilliant idea of the revolving bookcase which can still be seen in the house.

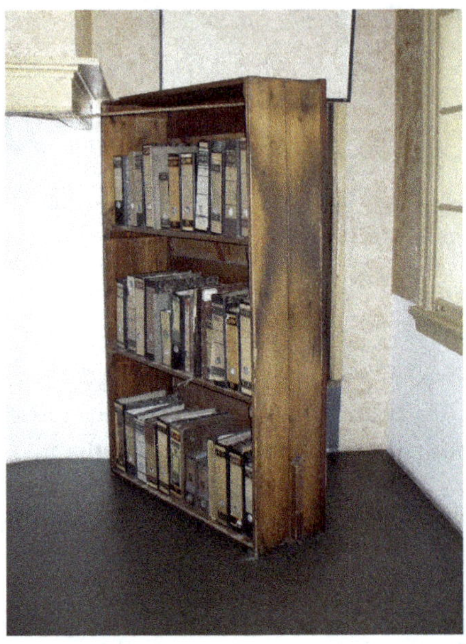

Revolving bookcase, photograph by Bungle, Wikimedia Commons

THE 'ACHTERHUIS'

Canal houses in Amsterdam sometimes had houses at the back, fully independent premises that could be reached by an alley. The Frank family moved to such an 'Achterhuis' (backhouse) on Prinsengracht 263, where Otto Frank had his businesses. Opekta sold ingredients for the manufacturing of jams and Pectacon sold spices for meat amongst others.

Shortly after they moved in, four others joined them: the Van Pels Family, father, mother and son. Hermann van Pels was one of Otto Frank's employees and an expert in herbs and spices. He was married to the elegant German lady Auguste. The last one, Miep Gies's dentist Fritz Pfeffer, originally from Berlin, joined them in November 1942. Much to her annoyance, Anne had to share her room with Fritz, who made odd noises while he slept. In total, they were with eight people.

Anne about the Achterhuis:

> "The Annex is an ideal place to hide in. It may be damp and lopsided, but there's probably not a more comfortable hiding place in all of Amsterdam. No, in all of Holland."

She loved the sound of the clocks from the nearby Westertoren that she heard every 15 minutes.

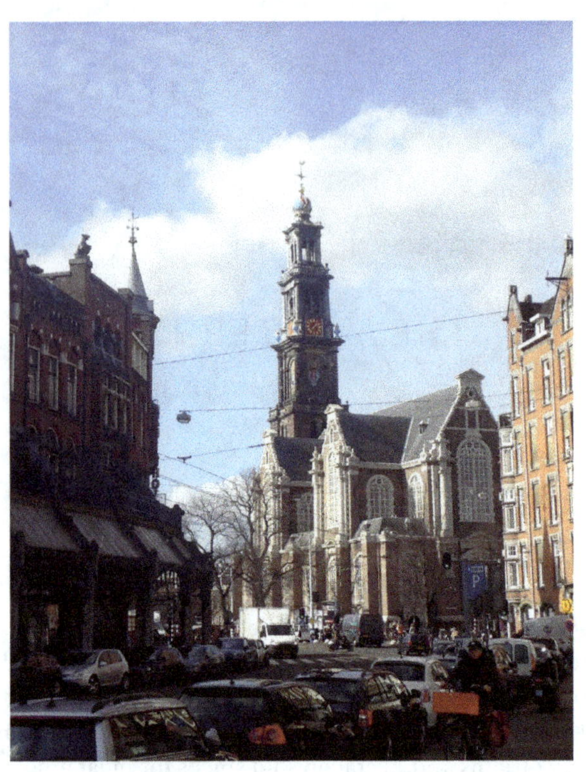

Westertoren in Amsterdam (photo by Publisher)

DAILY LIFE IN THE SECRET ANNEX

Since the families were confined to 75 square meters, they needed a tight schedule dictated by time-slots. During the day they had to be as silent as a mouse because of people in the office downstairs. Curtains had to be kept closed at all times. It was a damp and rather oppressive place to be, especially since several people smoked. Coughing, laughing or sneezing were forbidden, and all of them wore slippers to avoid making noises. Their biggest fear was getting ill and tried to keep fit by doing gymnastics during the first year into hiding. Their daily routine was scheduled around the office hours and the movements of the staff and clients downstairs; the toilet could only be flushed outside office hours.

Otto Frank had tried to obtain visas for him and his family to get to the United States, but this had been unsuccessful.

Since the Frank family were entirely dependent on their helpers, the situation got serious when the office clerks were ill or were otherwise unable to come and bring food. There were times that they had to eat the same meal for weeks on end. Anne wrote in het diary in May 1944 that vegetables were still very hard to come by. They had to eat 'rotten boiled lettuce', and added rather sarcastically:

'Add to that rotten potatoes and you have a meal fit for a king.'

Reading and studying were their main pastime. Otto Frank was an avid

Charles Dickens reader and was always immersed in his novels whilst looking up words he did not know. His wife Edith followed an English language course. The quiet and studious Margot Frank, did a Latin correspondence course, and read various kinds of books. Anne also spent her time reading and wrote in her diary.

At 6.45 am they all got up and got ready for the day before the office downstairs opened. By the time office staff arrived at 7.30 am they were all washed and started reading and studying in total silence. During noon they could relax a bit since the warehouse workers went home for lunch. The helpers often came to see them during lunch and brought supplies. Bep brought the daily groceries, and Miep usually provided books and food. Jan Gies, Miep's husband who worked at the city of Amsterdam and was a member of the resistance, helped with ration coupons.

At 1 pm they listened to the BBC radio from London. At 9 pm everybody prepared for bed. Anne, who always wanted to look her very best, got a time slot of half an hour for her beauty routine. She would comb her hair, while wearing a special pink robe, do her nails, or bleach her moustache. Every day she wanted to look her very best. After dinner they would sometimes play a game. Sleeping for Anne was difficult at times, especially when she heard shooting. It was a challenge for the lively, outgoing Anne. Keeping a diary was her life line.

THE BETRAYAL

An informant (the identity of whom is still unknown) betrayed them by revealing their hiding place, whereupon the German *Sicherheitsdienst* in the person of Karl Silberbauer and some Dutch police offers raided the house on Friday 4 August 1944.

After 2 years and 30 days in hiding, the Frank family were discovered and were arrested. Because Otto Frank had served during WWI, they were given a little more time to pack their belongings.

Via Westerbork, the Dutch transit camp, they were all transported to Auschwitz in Poland. The journey took 3 days and 3 nights; it was to be the very last train that would leave Westerbork for Auschwitz. Circumstances in the wagons were appalling. Although this has not been confirmed, Mrs van Pels appears to have died during the trip. Her dead body seems to have been thrown out of the train.

At Auschwitz, the men had to work in the gravel pits and work at road construction. Herman van Pels was sent to the gas chambers when he was no longer useful after having wounded his hand. Fritz Pfeffer was put on a transport to Neuengamme where he died in December 1944, and Peter van Pels died in Mauthausen at the age of eighteen.

Anne and Margot would be in Auschwitz for two month. At the end of 1944 they were transported to Bergen-Belsen, a camp without gas chambers.

They were in Bergen-Belsen during the winter of 1944-45, one of the severest in recent history. They had to live in cramped quarters, and subsequently in tents in the freezing cold. There was no sanitation, no water, and hardly any food.

In Bergen-Belsen Anne ran into two of her old friends from Amsterdam: Nanette Konig and Hannah Goslar. These friends both survived and could tell about the last days of Anne.

In January 2018 Nanette Blitz Konig published her memoirs and talks about her very last meeting with Anne Frank at Bergen-Belsen in: *Holocaust Memoirs by a Bergen-Belsen survivor & Classmate of Anne Frank*. Nanette and Anne wept for joy when they met. Anne was wrapped in a blanket because she could not stand her own clothes that were full of lice. She was trembling with cold and shivering, and was no longer the lively, strong girl that Nanette knew from their time together in Amsterdam. Anne was frightened and was not aware of the fact that her father was still alive. It was here at their very last meeting that Anne told Nanette what she had in mind with her diaries.

Anne, aged 15, and Margot, aged 19, died of typhus in March 1945, within a few days of each other. First Margot, then Anne, and only weeks before the Bergen-Belsen camp was to be liberated by the English troops. They had come so close to surviving the war and being reunited with their father.

Otto Frank was the only family member to survive the war. When Auschwitz was liberated by the Russian army in March 1945 Otto Frank was there. He had not been well enough to march and was left behind by the Germans. It took him half a year to get back to Amsterdam.

The liberation for Anne's mother came too late. Edith Frank had died of exhaustion and starvation in Auschwitz in January 1945, a few weeks before the liberation.

THE DIARIES

Before becoming a hideaway, Anne Frank had already shown ambition to become a writer and journalist. On her thirteenth birthday Otto Frank had given his youngest daughter her first diary. She started using it in 1942 and kept writing during the years in her hiding place.

Several diaries exist.

- Diary 1: 12 June 1942 - 5 December 1942,
- Diary 2: 22 December 1943 - 17 April 1944.

She probably had another diary that was used between 5 December 1942 and 22 December, but this one is lost. And her final diary,

- Diary 3: 17 April 1944 - 1 August 1944. She partly rewrote her first diaries onto loose sheets.

Anne describes her dreams, her fights with her parents and her emotional conflicts. Not only is the subject of her writing personal and direct, Anne Frank also shows an exceptional talent. The book is more than just a school girl writing about feelings and boys. It is literature by a promising young author: witty, energetic and with sharp insight into the people around her.

Anne planned to publish her diary as a novel after the war. The title she had in mind was 'Het Achterhuis'. Friends have described her as being full of life, chattery and think she would have loved being a famous writer..

Miep Gies and Bep Voskuijl, two of the office clerks and secret helpers of the family, had found the diaries in the ransacked house and kept them safe at their homes. Eventually, they wanted to give them back to Anne in case she survived the camps. That did not happen.

Otto Frank was given Anne's diaries, and granted his daughter's wish to have them published. It appears that Anne wrote for the last time three days before the arrest. In 1947, a first edition was printed after which more editions and translations followed. In 1963, Otto Frank founded the Anne Frank Foundation, a worldwide anti-racism organisation. It took a long time before Karl Josef Silberbauer was traced, which was due to Otto Frank's forgiveness.

The diaries are not the only manuscripts Anne Frank wrote. In 2004 the *Book of Beautiful Phrases* was published. It contains fragments from books and poems Anne liked and copied out. She also wrote her own poetry and *Little Stories And Events From The Annexe*.

SOME FACTS AND FIGURES

In total some 6 million Jews were killed during the Second World War. At the outbreak of the war, an estimated 140,000 Jews were living in The Netherlands, the majority of which lived in Amsterdam. Around 100,000 of them never returned from the camps. A small proportion of the Jewish population managed to survive by going into hiding. Some two-thirds of the 25,000 Jews who went into hiding survived.

Many books have been written about the Dutch during the war, and focus on the question how so many Jews could be deported while the Dutch looked on. Were they aware of what was going on in the camps? What did they do to prevent the deportations?

From her diary, we know that Anne guessed what was going on. On 9 October 1942 she wrote about the deportations, and the brutal way the Gestapo dealt with the Jews, transporting them in cattle wagons to Westerbork, the large transit camp in Drenthe.

She wondered what the situation was like in the concentration camps, and was aware of the gas chambers because of the daily radio broadcasts by the BBC. "Perhaps", she writes, "that is the quickest method of dying."

HISTORY OF THE ANNE FRANK HOUSE

After the Second World War, Otto Frank continued his business. He retired in 1956 and sold his office at Prinsengracht 263. The new owners planned to demolish the building. Public outrage over this plan was so fierce that it was decided to donate the building to the city. Led by Mayor Gijs van Hall, the people of Amsterdam raised funds to buy the house and surrounding buildings to be turned into a museum. In 1960, the Anne Frank House opened its doors. One of the wings of the museum was converted into a dormitory for students following summer courses in Amsterdam.

In 1997, the museum needed to expand because of the increasing number of visitors. Also, facilities had to be modernised. The students' dorms were replaced. It houses the bookshop and modern exhibition spaces.

The office and hiding place were restored to their original state. The office has a brick floor like in the 1930s. The original furniture has been put back in Otto Frank's office, alongside a glass door opening onto the room of Miep Gies. In the hiding place, walls are covered with copies of pictures that Anne Frank had glued on the wall herself.

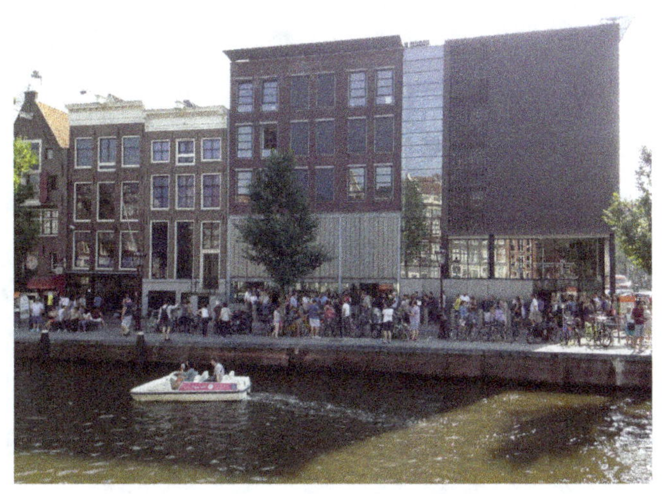

Anne Frank House in Amsterdam, Picture by the Publisher

THE ANNE FRANK TREE

Possibly the most famous tree in European history, the Anne Frank tree was the chestnut tree that features prominently in Anne's diary. Each day, Anne would go to the attic to blow the stuffy air out of her lungs and would look out at the tree, the sky and the birds gliding on the wind. She wrote she wouldn't be unhappy – if she were to live - as long as the tree existed with its branches and its shiny raindrops. For a moment, she would not feel like a caged bird.

This chestnut tree would become a symbol. When the borough of Amsterdam announced in 2007 that they would cut it down – it was infested with fungus - the announcement met with great resistance. The tree was so much more than a horse-chestnut tree. It was a symbol of the Holocaust. Worldwide protests, a foundation especially raised to protect the tree, and an iron structure costing €50.000, were all to no avail. In August 2010 it was blown over in a storm. Pieces of the tree were sold for large sums of money. Eleven saplings from the tree have since been distributed amongst museums and centers across the United States.

Anne Frank is not only the symbol of the pointlessness of war and destruction. She inspires people to live their lives and exploit their talents, no matter the circumstances.

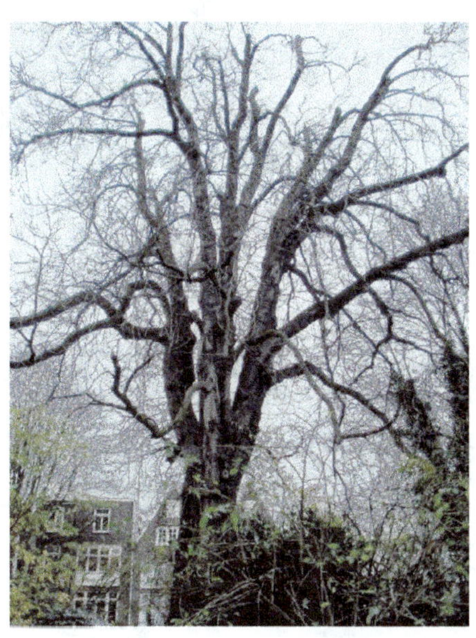

*Dying Chestnut Tree, Photograph by huliana90212, edited by
Arthena, via Wikimedia Commons*

LOCATION AND ADDRESS

For many visitors the Anne Frank House is an emotional experience. Therefore, please bear in mind that taking photographs or videos is not allowed. Moreover, the rooms and passageways are small and taking photographs will cause obstruction. Don't take a backpack or any big bag. The museum does not have a cloakroom.

There are always huge long queues in front of the museum. If you can, do book your tickets in advance! To avoid the queue, you can book tickets online or reserve a time of arrival. You print them out, and go straight to the special entrance to the left of the main entrance. This is the most convenient way, and it saves you a lot of queuing time.

Ticket sales

Address: The Anne Frank House is situated in the centre of Amsterdam at Prinsengracht 263-267. It takes around 20 minutes to walk from Amsterdam Central Station to the museum. Trams 13, 14 and 17 and buses 170, 172 and 174 stop nearby, at the 'Westermarkt' stop.

Do not wait until you are in Amsterdam to make the booking as the tickets sell out quickly in high season. Book them before you leave for your visit to Amsterdam.

The museum has extended opening hours in July and August: 9 am - 10 pm. During the year the museum is open 9 am - 7 pm, and on Saturdays 9 am - 9 pm.

In case it is impossible to book in advance, then try to visit the museum in the evening. Last entrance: 30 minutes before closing time.

TIP: It is recommended to have a look at the Anne Frank House website because they have a great 3-D reconstruction of the annex which gives a good idea of the rooms.

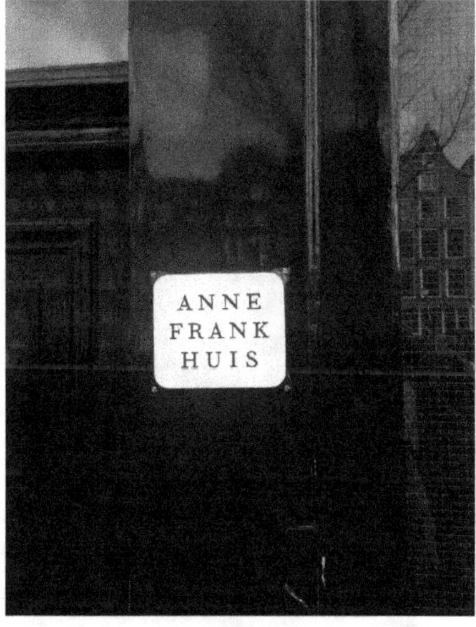

Plaquette at the Anne Frank House, Picture by the Publisher

MUSEUMS NEAR THE ANNE FRANK HOUSE

The Anne Frank House is close to Dam Square in the centre of town. Two other museums are located on this square.

The Royal Palace is open on a limited number of days during the year. Originally constructed as Amsterdam's town hall in the 17th century, it has beautifully decorated halls, and an exquisite collection of Empire Furniture.

The Royal Palace Amsterdam is one of the three palaces officially used by the Dutch Royal House. The Palace in Amsterdam is used for State Visits, the King's New Year receptions and many other official functions. During the period around these events the Palace is closed to the public.

New Church (Dutch: 'Nieuwe Kerk') next to the Royal Palace is the church where Dutch Kings and Queens are inaugurated. It houses temporary exhibitions, mostly art works from exotic cultures.

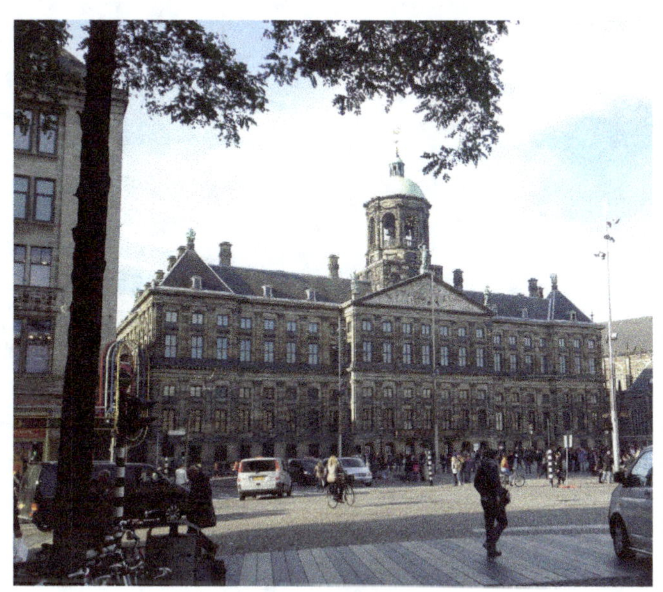

The Royal Palace, Amsterdam

You may find these memoirs interesting. It is the autobiography written by one of Anne Frank's classmates at the Jewish school in Amsterdam, Nanette Blitz Konig. She was one of the last people to see Anne alive at Bergen-Belsen.

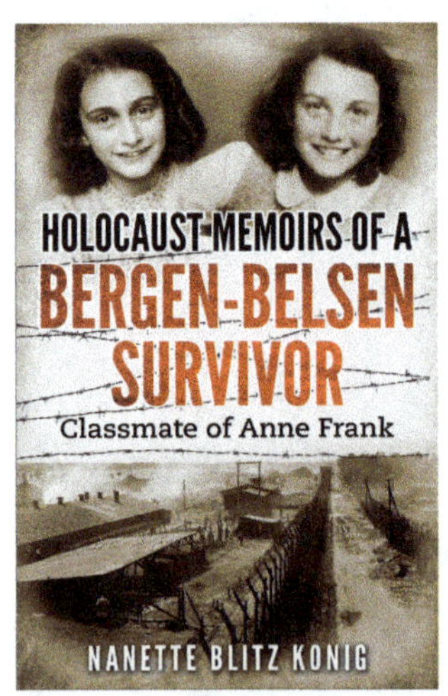

VAN GOGH MUSEUM

HIGHLIGHTS OF THE COLLECTION

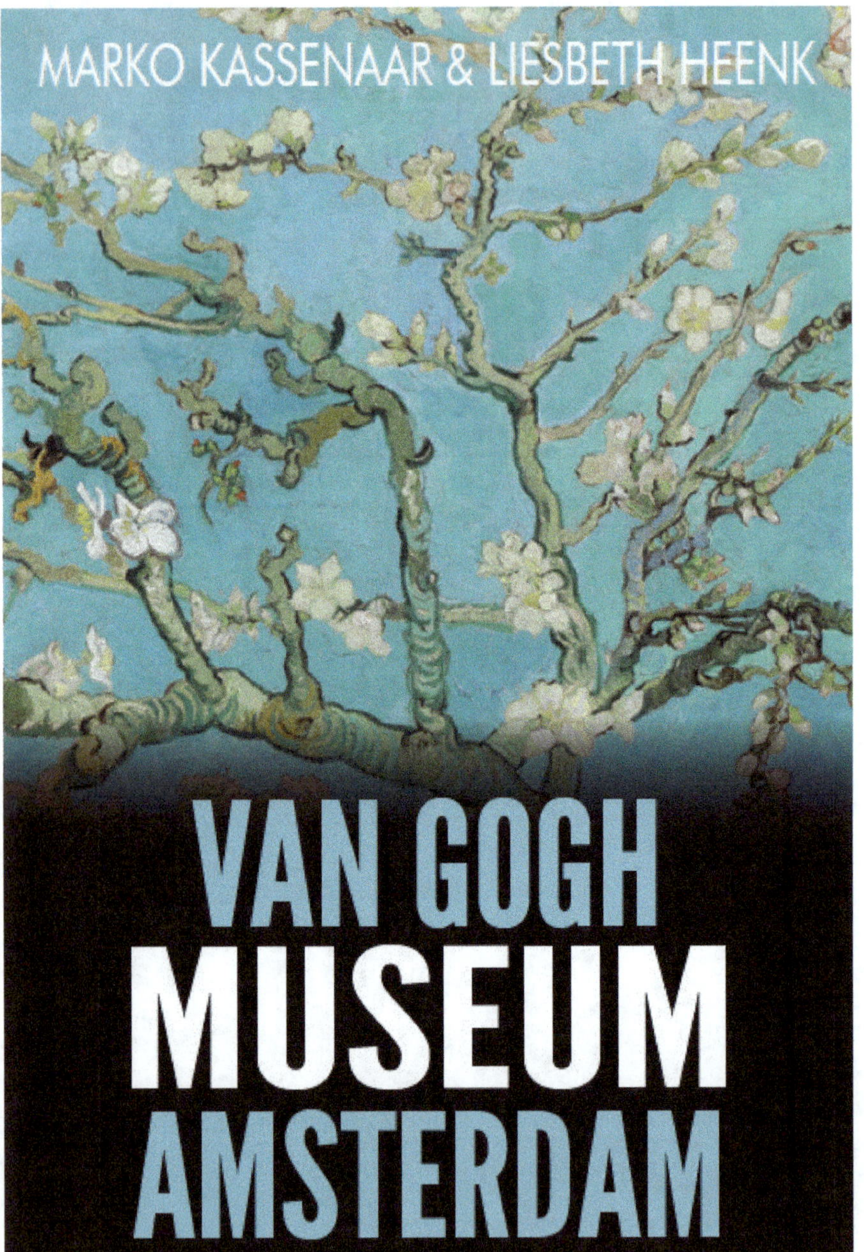

MARKO KASSENAAR & LIESBETH HEENK
VAN GOGH
MUSEUM
AMSTERDAM

INTRODUCTION

In this volume you will be introduced to Van Gogh's masterpieces, and you will discover some of the ideas and ambitions behind his art. For the purpose of clarity we will stick to a chronological presentation, while discussing works by Van Gogh and by other artists separately.

The Van Gogh museum houses the world's largest Van Gogh collection, comprising some 200 paintings, 400 drawings and 700 letters.

On display along with these works are masterpieces by Van Gogh's contemporaries, including Paul Gauguin, Emile Bernard, Georges Seurat, Camille Pissarro, Paul Signac and Auguste Rodin.

When Vincent van Gogh died in 1890, he did not leave a will. The artist's three sisters Elisabeth, Anna and Willemien decided that all of Van Gogh's work would be inherited by Theo, who after all took care of him during his entire career. Thus, the entire collection of Van Gogh paintings, drawings and letters were owned by Van Gogh's brother Theo.

After Theo's death, on 25 January 1891, it passed to his widow, Johanna van Gogh-Bonger (1862-1925). She sold some of the works, but the majority stayed in her possession and were inherited by her son, Vincent Willem van Gogh (1890-1978) in 1925. Part of the works she sold are now in the wonderful collection of the Kröller-Müller museum in The Netherlands. This museum, set in a beautiful park, holds the second largest collection of Van Goghs in the world, and is definitely worthwhile a visit.

Vincent, an engineer, loaned some of his uncle's works to the Stedelijk Museum, Amsterdam's premier venue for modern art, in 1930. As the appreciation for the works of the artist Vincent van Gogh exploded, the demand grew for a special museum. At that time, a museum dedicated to a single artist was still something of an anomaly.

A foundation was set up in order to keep Van Gogh's unsold paintings and drawings, but also other artists' work as well as the book and print collections, together as one collection. Various paintings by Van Gogh's friends and contemporaries were part of the collection of contemporary art owned by Vincent and his brother Theo van Gogh.

In 1962, the collection was put in the care of the foundation for 15 million guilders, even though the estimated value of the collection was more than 300 million guilders.

The Dutch state built the Van Gogh Museum and still acts as the collection's administrator. Legally, the collection is on permanent loan to the Dutch state.

In 1973 Queen Juliana of the Netherlands opened the Van Gogh Museum, housed in the same specially designed building that it occupies today.

The collection has substantially grown since the inauguration of the museum, and through the financial support of the Vincent van Gogh Foundation, the Prince Bernhard Fund and many other sponsors, new works of exceptional standing have been acquired. The museum regularly exhibits long-term loans from other institutions.

THE BUILDING

The original museum building is designed by one of the most prominent members of the Dutch artistic movement *De Stijl*, the architect Gerrit Rietveld.

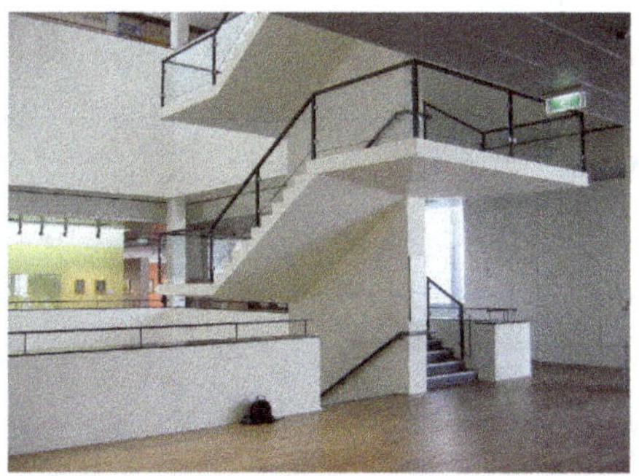

Japanese Wing of the Van Gogh Museum, main building., designed by Gerrit Rietveld. Photography by Minke Wagenaar – Wikimedia Commons.

Unfortunately, Rietveld was not able to fully realize his vision, as he died before the completion of the building in 1973. Still, with its clear lines and walls devoid of embellishment, enabling the visitor to focus entirely on the paintings themselves, the Van Gogh Museum is characteristic of Rietveld who was famous for his simplified creations.

The annex was designed by the architect Kisho Kurokawa (1934 - 2007) and built in 1999. It is known as the Kurokawa wing, and is used for temporary exhibitions.

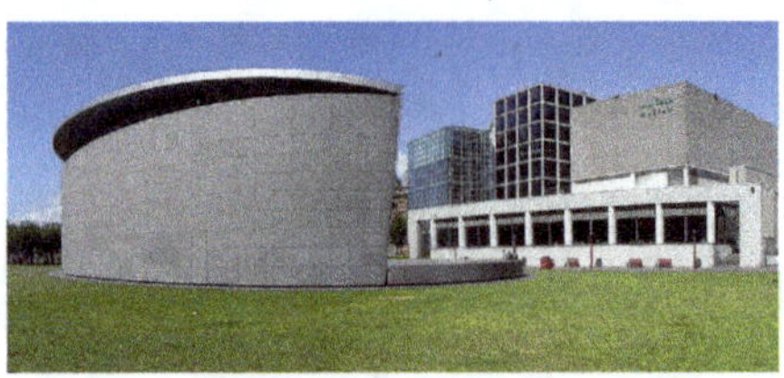

The Kurokawa wing of the Van Gogh Museum. Photography by Wladislav – Wikimedia Commons.

More recent alterations to the building include the construction of a new entrance hall. Since September 2015, visitors enter the museum through a glass building on Museumplein. The new transparent structure gave the museum another 800 square meters, improving the experience for the ever growing number of visitors. . Due to time-slotted admission tickets, visitor do not perceive the museum as overcrowded, even in the rather busy summer months. There is a new spacious and light reception area with cloakrooms, and a completely redesigned museum shop.

Having long been a dream of the museum, the new entrance hall was designed by Kisho Kurokawa Architect & Associates from Tokyo, the same agency that worked on the annex.

The Van Gogh Museum is one of the most popular museums in Amsterdam. In 2017 the total number of visitor was 2.26 million, coming from over 125 countries in the world.

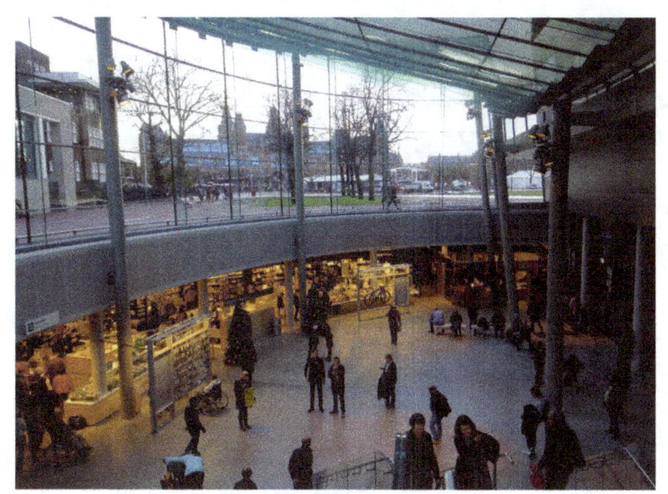

*Interior of the new entrance hall with the Rijksmuseum in the
back. Picture by the Publisher.*

SHORT BIOGRAPHY OF VINCENT VAN GOGH

When comparing Vincent van Gogh's career with those of other artists, it soon becomes clear that his was one of the shortest in art history. It was not until the age of twenty-seven that he began work as a full-time professional painter, and he died a mere ten years later.

Yet in this short window of time, Vincent van Gogh (1853 - 1890) produced a body of works that is not only impressive in size, but also marks the origin of several modern art movements.

From the years following his death up until present day, artists have been inspired by his vibrant and innovative use of color, his expressionism, as well as his uncompromising attitude towards art and life.

Born in the small town of Groot-Zundert (Brabant) in The Netherlands in 1853, Vincent Willem van Gogh was a shy and introverted child. At the age of sixteen he began work as an assistant at the art dealership Goupil & Co. in The Hague, a company his brother Theo would also join a few years later.

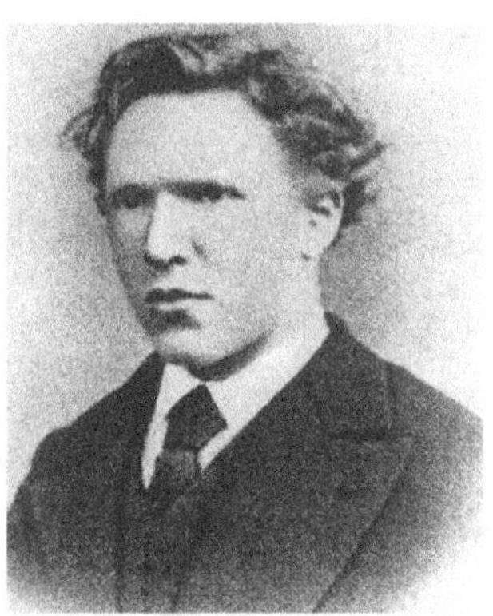

Vincent van Gogh, 18 years old.

During this time, Van Gogh was reassigned to various major cities including London and Paris, before eventually losing his job in 1876. Although he loved art, he did not especially like his job in the art world. After his dismissal, he took an unpaid job at a boarding school in Ramsgate (England). Various other jobs followed, not terribly successful. In 1878 he relocated to Belgium to work as a layman minister, and ended up realizing his artistic calling.

Van Gogh's career properly began in 1880, after he had moved back to The Netherlands where he hoped to find work as an illustrator for magazines and newspapers.

The first years were difficult and consisted of endless studying and copying prints. Unfortunately he lacked an innate talent, so it took considerable time before he could draw properly; Van Gogh was incapable of drawing 'from nature'. He needed an object in front of him, but even then, the result was awkward. More often than not the postures of his figures were rather wooden, with arms and legs being out of proportion.

The Hague period saw some touching drawings of figures, and the highlight of his Dutch years, *The Potato Eaters,* was made in Nuenen (Brabant) in 1885. After a short period of studying art in Antwerp, Van Gogh decided to go to Paris to live with his brother, who had by then become manager of Goupil & Co.

It was in Paris that Van Gogh developed the personal style that would epitomize his work. Influenced by impressionism, he experimented with vivid colors and expressive brushstrokes, and he also discovered a new source of inspiration in the plethora of Japanese art that was entering the capital at this time.

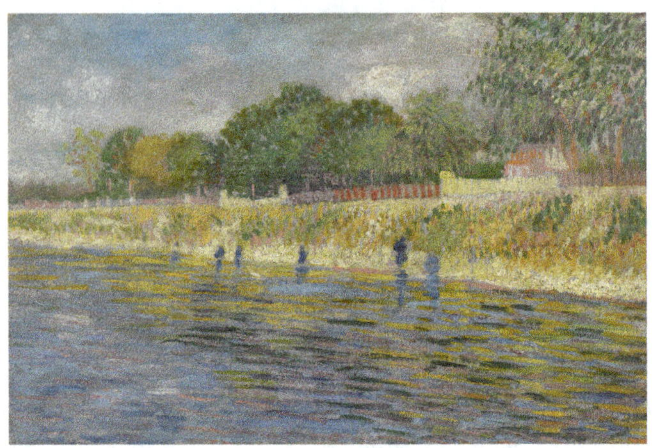

Vincent van Gogh, Bank of the Seine, oil on canvas, May - July 1887

Noise, temptation and the bustle of city life began took their toll on Van Gogh. Anxious, stressed and in the early stages of alcoholism, he escaped to the tranquillity of Arles in southern France. The artist also hoped that life would be less expensive in the country. It was in Arles that he painted his most iconic works, such as *The Sunflowers* and his own bedroom in the Yellow House.

Already suffering from a deteriorating mental illness, Van Gogh began to experience epileptic seizures. Living together with Paul Gauguin in the Yellow House in Arles ended in disaster; in December 1888 he dramatically cut off his left ear and was hospitalized.

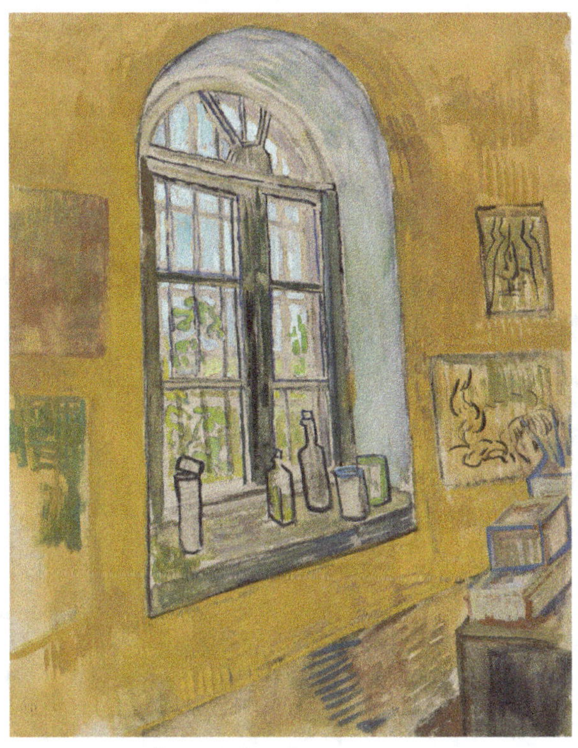

Vincent van Gogh, Window in the Studio, mixed media on paper,
September – October 1889

The unique discovery of a doctor's letter containing information about the cut-off ear aroused great interest in 2016. It showed that he did not simply cut off an earlobe, as was hitherto thought, but his entire ear.

The combination of his illness and fierce temper meant that the villagers began to fear him. The artist felt he was unable to live on his own, and volunteered to be admitted to an asylum in Saint-Rémy.

He stayed in the asylum of Saint-Paul for two years where he was allowed to work in an empty room that he used as studio. It was a period of great distress; he had various epileptic seizures and he feared that the time would eventually come that he would be unable to paint or draw. That, of course, was his biggest fear. At the same time it was also a period during which his star began to rise; articles about Van Gogh's work were starting to appear. Upon being released from the asylum, Van Gogh moved to Auvers-sur-Oise, near Paris. There, the local Dr. Gachet would look after him.

In this village, Van Gogh painted his final works before his tragic death on 29th July 1890. Dying from a bullet wound to the chest, it seems plausible that Van Gogh shot himself. The revolver with which Van Gogh seems to have fatally wounded himself was found in Auvers in 2016.

Buried in Auvers-sur-Oise, Van Gogh was not alone for long, since his brother Theo came to share his resting place only six months later.

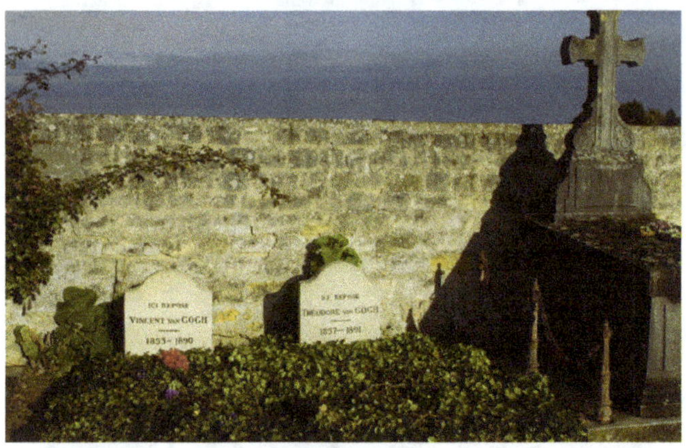

The graves of Vincent van Gogh and Theo van Gogh in Auvers-sur-Oise

PERMANENT COLLECTION

In November 2014 the Van Gogh Museum redesigned the presentation of its permanent collection, putting more emphasis on what draws people from all over the world to the museum: the artist's tortured life.

The museum nowadays focuses on the complete story: the artist, the context, Van Gogh's personal ambitions, his emotions, the many myths and his influence on other artists.

If you enter the museum you will be face to face with larger than life blow-ups of the artist's multi-colored self-portrait and half a dozen of painted self-portraits. This is the right choice: we, the public, are very much interested in getting to know the man Van Gogh.

In the presentation Van Gogh's paintings have been given ample space, and the walls vary in color. They have chosen a greyish-brown for the early Brabant paintings and drawings, a green-blue for the Paris pictures, a rich blue for his dazzling works from Provence, and various subtle greens and blues for his other works. Because of the fragility of works on paper, a changing selection of only a few drawings are being displayed.

Although the display is basically chronological, the work has been arranged according to certain themes. As a visitor you can follow the on-going search of this extraordinary artist. Issues are being discussed such as the ear incident, the suicide and the mental illness, death and recognition, the discoloration of his paintings and the origins of the Van Gogh museum. At the very end of the presentation, on the top floor of the building, a gallery displays work by Van Gogh's followers.

THE NETHERLANDS

Not only is *The Potato Eaters* considered the artist's first masterpiece, it is also the largest work he ever painted. It portrays a peasant family, illuminated by a single lamp, with nothing except potatoes to eat for their dinner.

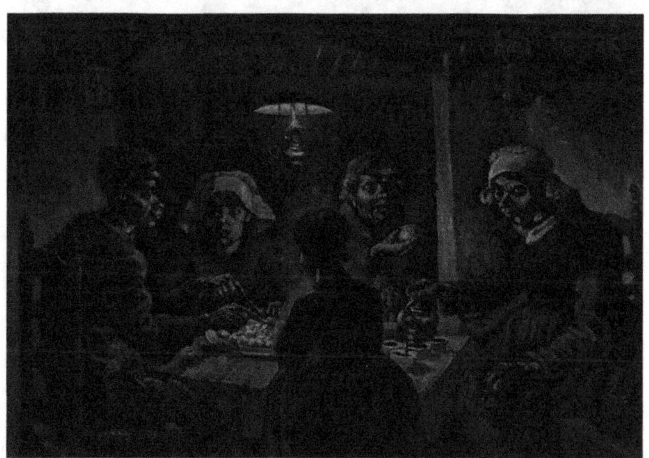

Vincent van Gogh, The Potato Eaters, oil on canvas, April - May
1885

To the right, a woman pours chicory, a cheap substitute for coffee. The hardened faces and muted colors suggest the burdens of life in the countryside.

By looking closely, one can make out a clock alongside a painting of the crucifixion in the background on the upper left. You may not see this on the reproduction, but you'll notice it in the museum.

Affected by his time as a lay preacher amongst the poor in the Borinage mining district of Belgium, Van Gogh was deeply sympathetic to the sufferings of common people.

The artist wrote to his brother Theo on 30 April 1885 that the painting had to express the idea that these farmers:

> "tilled the earth themselves with these hands they are putting in the dish,
> (...) and that they have thus honestly *earned* their food."

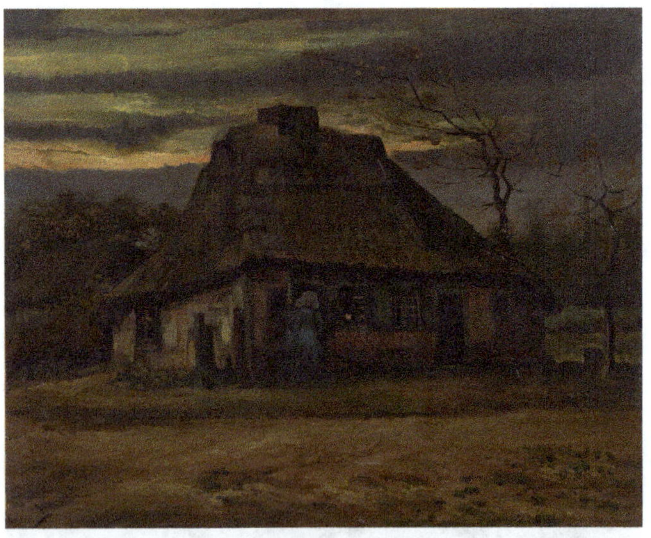

Vincent van Gogh, The cottage, oil on canvas, May 1885

Using farmers and laborers as his models, like Jules Breton and Jean-François Millet had done before him, the countryside was his preferred setting and subject. *The Potato Eaters* forms part of a series of works on this theme, using the dark colors that were popular in the Netherlands during this time.

ANTWERP (1885 - 1886)

Having employed dark, sombre colors for the majority of his early works, Van Gogh decided to brighten his palette and began to take courses at the art academy in Antwerp.

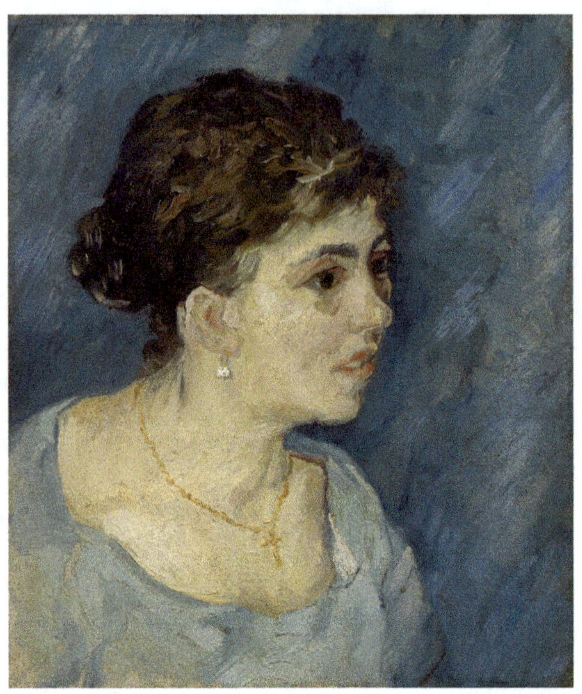

Vincent van Gogh, Portrait of a Prostitute, oil on canvas,
December 1885

The colors went from muted browns and grays to vibrant blues and rosy skin, and the brushstrokes became more refined.

Remaining poor throughout his life, Van Gogh often hired prostitutes, like the woman in this portrait, to sit for his paintings rather than professional models since they demanded a significantly lower fee.

As his art earned him no money, Van Gogh found himself financially dependent on his brother Theo. Theo fully supported him from 1882 onwards, agreeing that this arrangement would remain in place until the artist could support himself. This would never happen. (Cf *Van Gogh and Money. The Myth of the Poor Artist* by Liesbeth Heenk.)

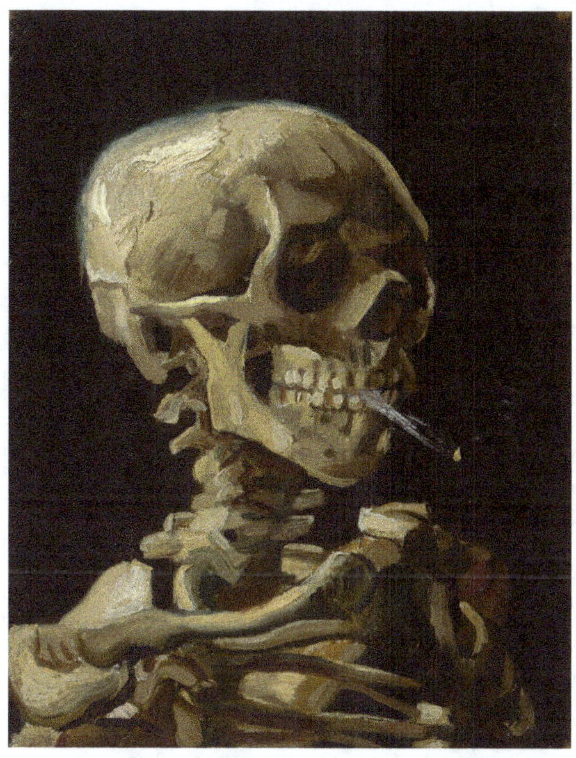

The *Head of a skeleton with a burning cigarette*, made in February 1886, is probably an ironic comment on the traditional training offered at the Antwerp academy where Van Gogh enrolled for a short course, and where he was criticized for painting 'too roughly'.

A skeleton would often be used in class to study human anatomy. Van Gogh used this familiar subject to make his own wry statement.

PARIS (1886 - 1888)

Paris signified a new life for Van Gogh. New influences from art movements like impressionism and pointillism transformed his way of working. The rough brushstrokes from his earlier Dutch works were replaced by dots and small stripes, and he used much lighter colors.

Like other Parisian painters of this period, Van Gogh painted people in natural settings, such as parks and gardens. This painting uses an old-fashioned composition as a model: the horizon is placed in the middle of the canvas, with one tree positioned exactly in the centre, and a pair of lovers depicted on either side.

Though this is not yet the work of an avant-garde artist such as his contemporaries Gauguin or Bernard, the magnificent colors reveal Van Gogh's development.

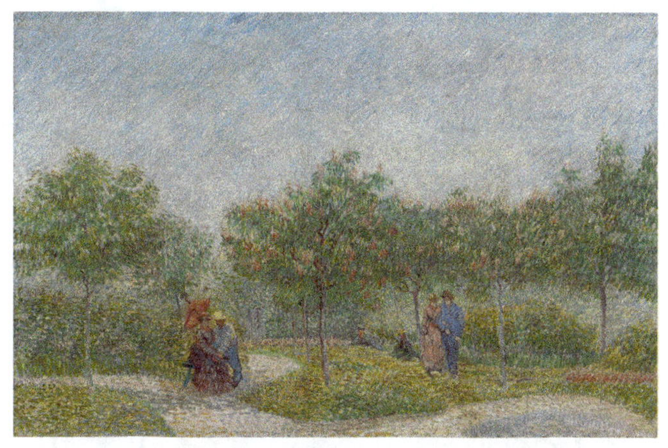

*Vincent van Gogh, Garden with Courting Couples: Square Saint-
Pierre, oil on canvas, May 1887*

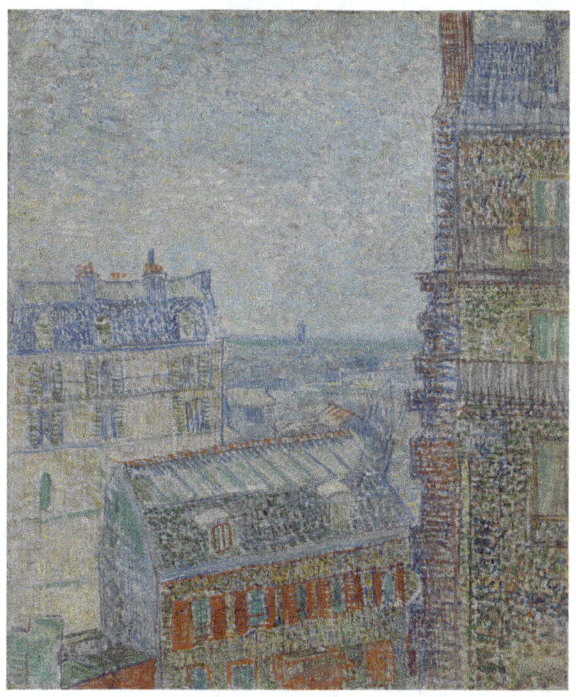

*Vincent van Gogh, View from Theo's apartment, oil on canvas,
March - April 1887*

When looking closely at *View from Theo's apartment*, one can see how Van

Gogh experimented with pointillism: the work is almost entirely made up of small dots, with lines being reserved for the contours of the houses.

This painting shows the view from the apartment shared by Van Gogh and Theo at 54, Rue Lepic, in the famous district of Montmartre.

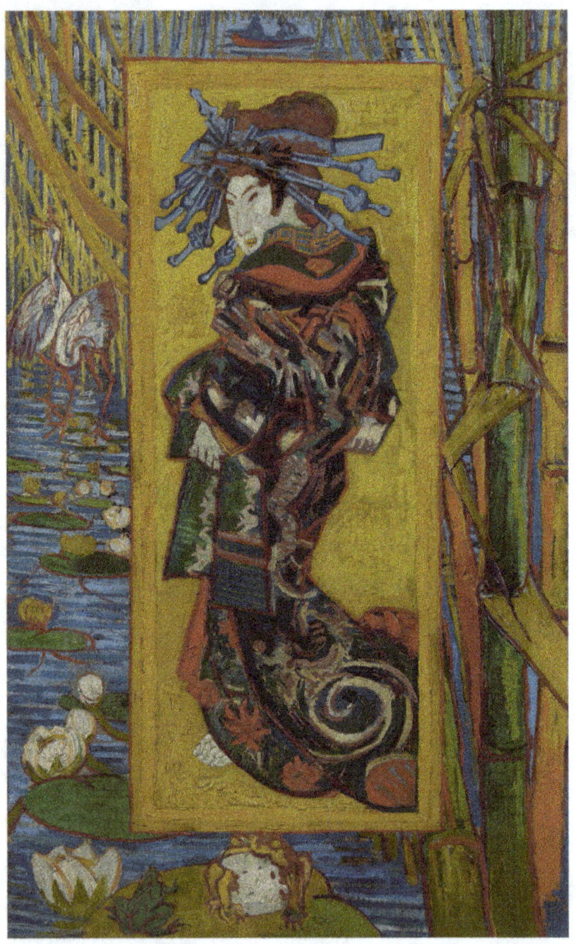

Vincent van Gogh, Courtesan (after Eisen), oil on canvas, October - November 1887

Van Gogh was fond of Japanese art, admiring the bright colors, clear contours and manner of composition. In *Courtesan*, he copied a portrait of a geisha from the cover of the *Paris Illustré* magazine. A geisha was a high-class courtesan who sometimes offered sexual favors.

In the background, Van Gogh has painted bamboo, frogs, canes and a small boat. The animals in particular were meant as a joke: the French words for crane ('grue') and frog ('grenouille') were also nicknames for a prostitute.

Bamboo frames the central image, magnified and placed in the foreground in a typically Japanese composition. Further back is a pond revealing small animals and lotus flowers dotted around the painting. In the work below, you can see another example of this type of composition.

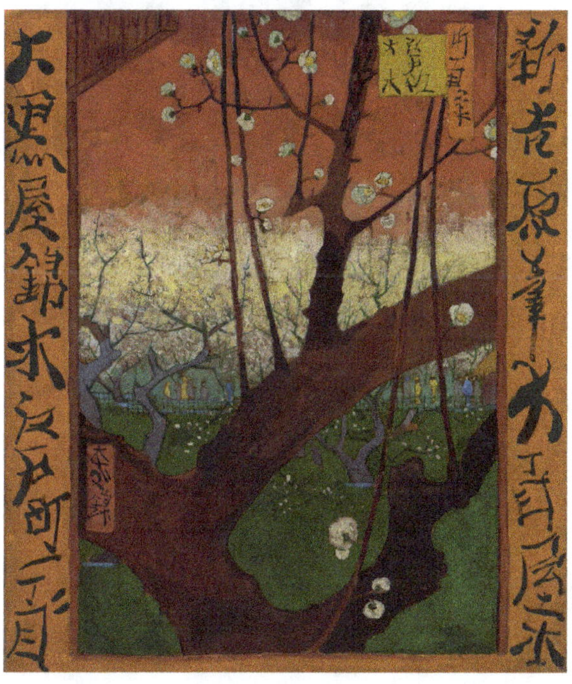

Vincent van Gogh, Flowering plum orchard (after Hiroshige), oil on canvas, October - November 1887

Van Gogh's japonaiserie also becomes clear in this painting of a garden. Like the bamboo in the image above, the tree is placed prominently in the foreground of this composition.

Close observation of the piece reveals a combination of styles, including the aforementioned Japanese composition which is combined with the impressionist brushstrokes of the blossoms in the background.

The borders are decorated with Japanese characters. Van Gogh was oblivious to their meaning, but copied the shapes simply liking the way they looked. The characters are actually an advertisement for a house up for a sale - including an address!

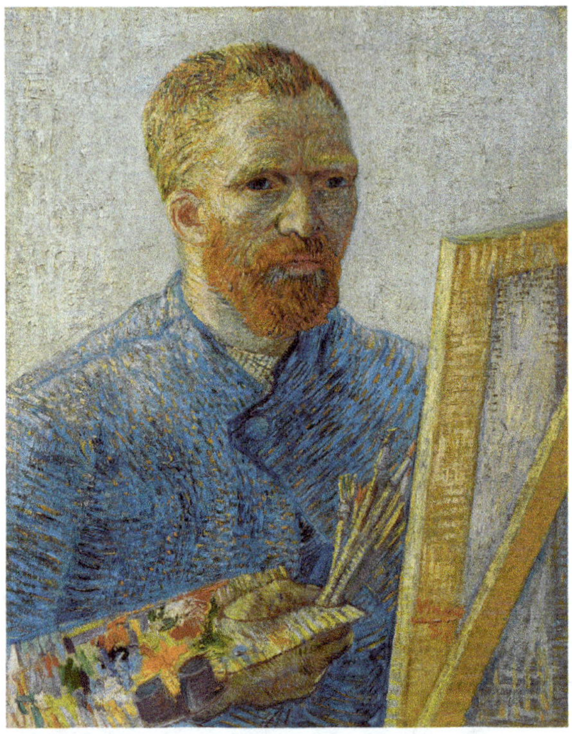

Van Gogh painted many self-portraits. This was not out of vanity, but lack of money: instead of spending the little money he had on models, he bought a small mirror.

In this painting, he confidently portrays himself as an artist with his tools. Though many of his self-portraits are rather unrefined, this one is worth a closer look since it is very detailed.

This becomes clear in the number of colors he mixed to paint his hair and eyes. Van Gogh must have been pleased with the result; he confidently signed the painting at the lower right.

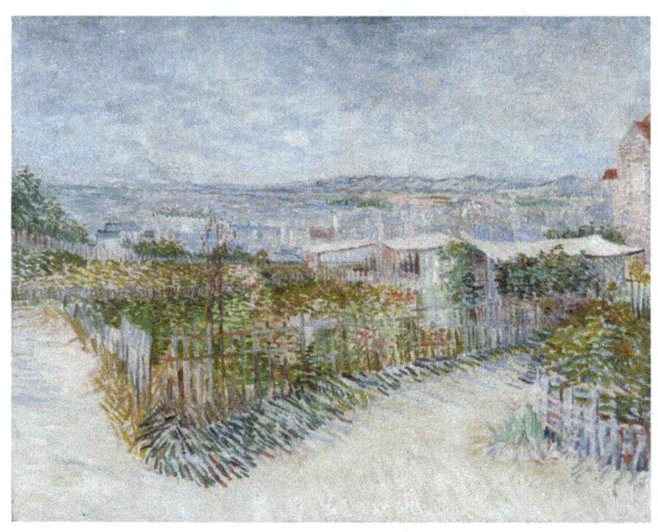

Vincent van Gogh, Montmartre: Behind the Moulin de la Galette,
oil on canvas, July 1887

Impressionist painters aimed to portray the first impressions of the eye. This had to be done quickly, before the movement of the sun altered the light of the landscape. Therefore, impressionist paintings were often produced very quickly, resulting in a sketch-like appearance.

This painting is an example of Van Gogh experimenting with this style. Impressionist painters did not mix their paint on the palette before applying it, instead mixing the colors *on* the canvas itself, producing a far more varied spectrum.

Evidence of this can be seen in the pink house to the right, which contrasts beautifully with the sky and sandy path.

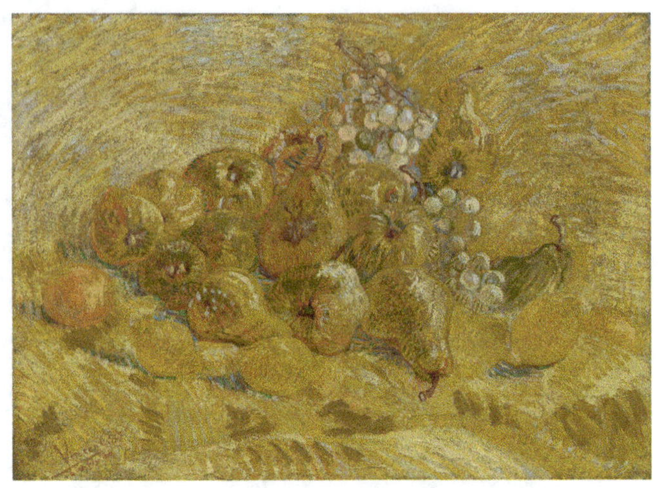

*Vincent van Gogh, Quinces, lemons, pears and grapes, oil on
canvas, October 1887*

In Paris Van Gogh made various still lifes. This still life combining grapes, pears and lemons, one can make out the many influences on Van Gogh. The impressionist effect is immediately visible in the depiction of the fruit: the shadows emphasizing the shapes are not black, but in yellow, orange and white. The background clashes with the subject of the painting in its completely different rhythm of brushstrokes.

Japanese elements can be seen in the flatness of the perspective - the entire composition is made up of a large yellow color plane. Moreover, the frame is decorated with shapes that look like Japanese characters. Van Gogh dedicated this painting to the most important person in his life. Under his signature in the left bottom corner, he has written 'à mon frère Theo' - 'to my brother Theo'.

ARLES (1888 - 1889)

After spending just two years in Paris, Van Gogh yearned for the countryside. He chose to move to Arles, where the strong sunlight makes all colors deeper and brighter. There he rented part of a house, depicted in *The Yellow House*, and dreamed of setting up a commune for artists.

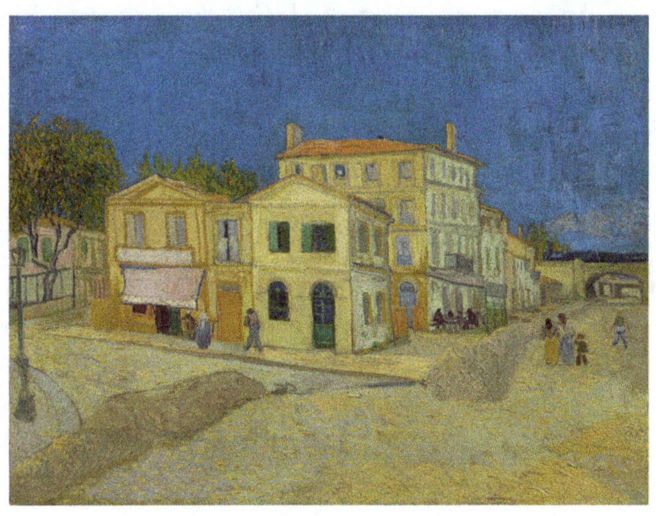

Vincent van Gogh, The Yellow House, oil on canvas, September 1888

The first painter to join Van Gogh in Arles was Paul Gauguin, an artist that he held in high esteem. Their collaboration lasted only nine weeks since they had many heated debates, ending with the infamous incident where Van Gogh cut off part of his earlobe. Interestingly, this was also the period when Van Gogh produced his greatest works.

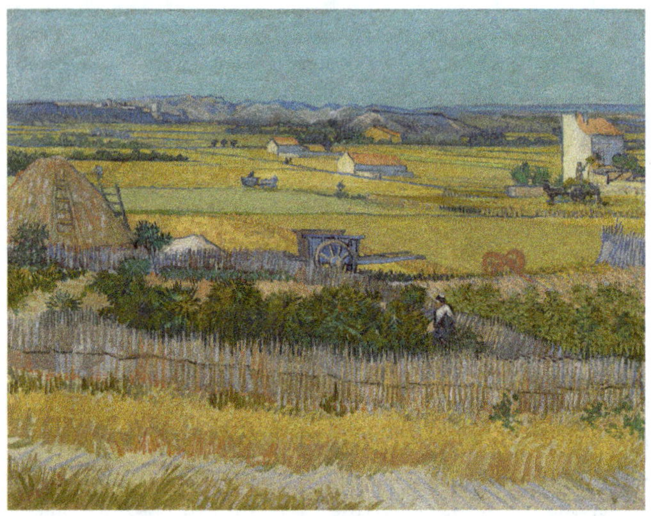

Vincent van Gogh, The Harvest at La Crau, oil on canvas, June 1888

This painting of a harvest is actually a Japanese-style French landscape. Comparing this work to the Parisian paintings of the geisha and the plum tree, strong similarities in both composition and color come to light.

Contrastingly, the cornfield is painted with impressionist dots and stripes. This is the magic of Van Gogh: he mixes different styles but the result is always genuinely his own.

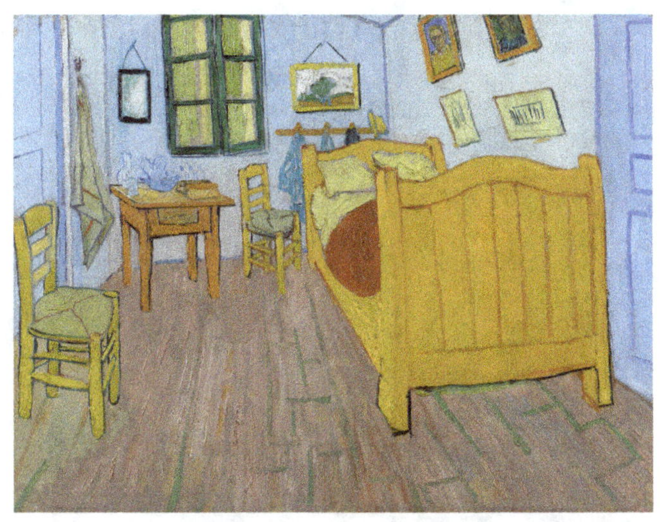

Vincent van Gogh, The Bedroom, oil on canvas, October 1888

Japanese influences are also visible in this famous painting of Van Gogh's bedroom. The perspective is not quite accurate, which was intentional.

In order to make it look more like a Japanese print, Van Gogh flattened the whole scene and left out all the shadows. You may recognize other Japanese elements like bright colors and clear contours.

It is clear from this painting that the painter's lifestyle was rather simple. Apart from the necessities, this sparse room does not include much, except for two simple chairs, a water bowl and paintings on the wall, including two portraits over his bed.

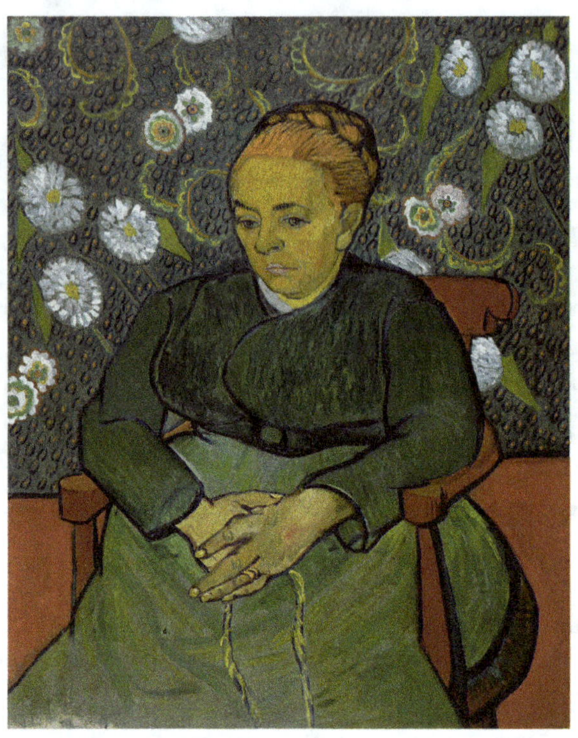

Vincent van Gogh, Augustine Roulin ("La berceuse"), oil on canvas, 1888

The woman portrayed here is Augustine Roulin, the wife of the postman Joseph Roulin, one of Van Gogh's closest friends in Arles. Her nickname 'la berceuse' means both 'lullaby' and 'babysitter' in French. This is alluded to by the cord in her hands, as it was used to rock the cradle while singing lullabies.

For Van Gogh, she was the ultimate symbol of comfort and motherhood. He planned to make a triptych using this painting as the middle panel, with pictures of sunflowers on either side. His intention was to combine motherly love with the beauty and power of nature.

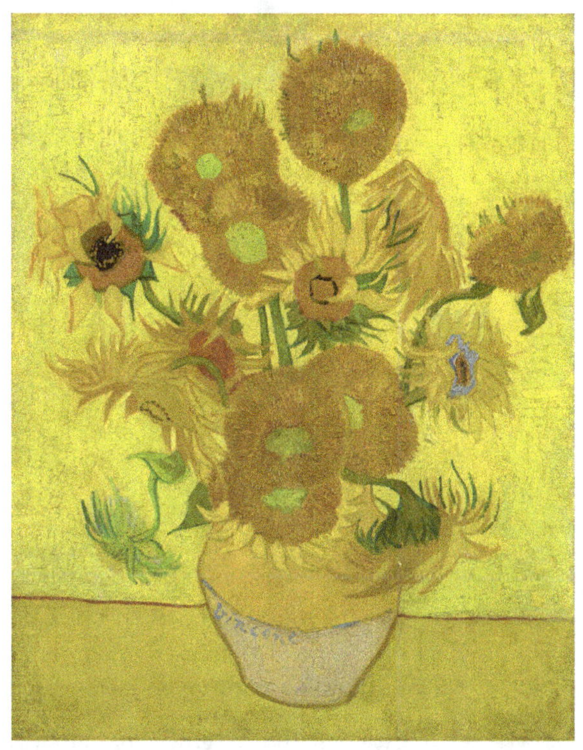

Vincent van Gogh, Sunflowers, oil on canvas, January 1889

Sunflower paintings are iconic of Van Gogh's *oeuvre*. In total, there are five different versions of this still life, and the Van Gogh Museum exhibits and owns the fifth and last of the series.

Van Gogh applied a vigorous energy to the painting of these flowers, and everything is imbued with a fierce yellow hue. The flowers are depicted through lumps of paint rather than brushstrokes.

Though originally conceived and designed as a side-panel for a painting that Van Gogh considered more important, the portrait of Augustine Roulin that is shown above, this painting is now perhaps the most famous of all of Van Gogh's works.

SAINT-RÉMY (1889 - 1890)

When Van Gogh was voluntarily admitted to the hospital in Saint-Rémy after cutting off his earlobe, he demanded an extra room to be able to work on his art. Beside his own paintings, he made copies of works that he loved.

Shown here is a Pietà, portraying the Virgin Mary mourning her son's death. This was made after a lithograph based on a painting by Eugène Delacroix (1798 - 1863).

By taking a closer look at the face of Jesus you may notice something familiar, as this is a self-portrait. Without a hint of arrogance, Van Gogh saw it as his way to identify with salvation and the end of suffering.

The painting actually is the result from a little accident. In his letter to Theo the artist wrote:

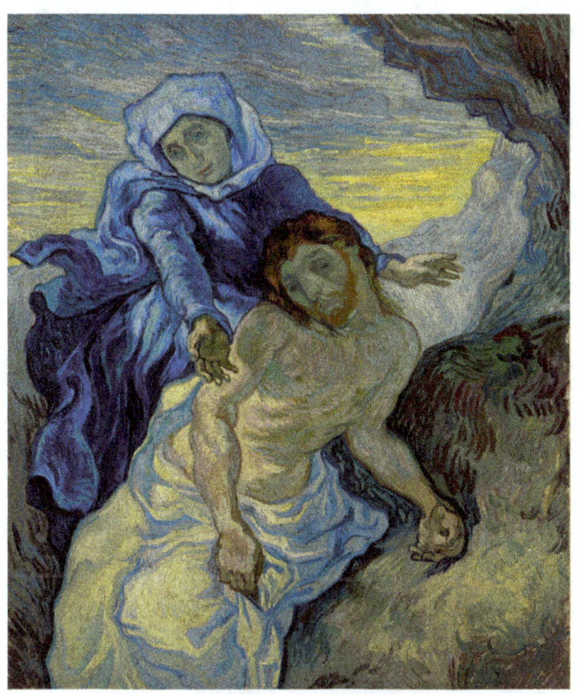

Vincent van Gogh, Pietà (after Delacroix), oil on canvas,
September 1889

"that lithograph of Delacroix, the Pietà, with other sheets had fallen into some oil and paint and got spoiled. I was sad about it – then in the meantime I occupied myself painting it, and you'll see it one day."

The lithograph has survived, with the stain still visible.

After recovering from his illness in April 1890, Van Gogh worked on a series of flower still lifes. The subject of one these paintings is a bouquet of bright blue irises, set against a strong yellow background.

Compared to his sunflowers, this image is more balanced with regard to color, as the purple / blue flowers and green stems lend the painting a lighter and less bold tone.

You should see the painting as a study in color. Van Gogh planned to achieve a powerful color contrast. By placing the purple flowers against a yellow background, he made the decorative forms stand out strongly.

Interestingly, the red pigment in the flowers has faded. The irises were originally purple, and have now turned blue.

Van Gogh made two paintings of this joyous bouquet. In the still life (in the Metropolitan Museum of Art) he experimented with combining purple, pink and green.

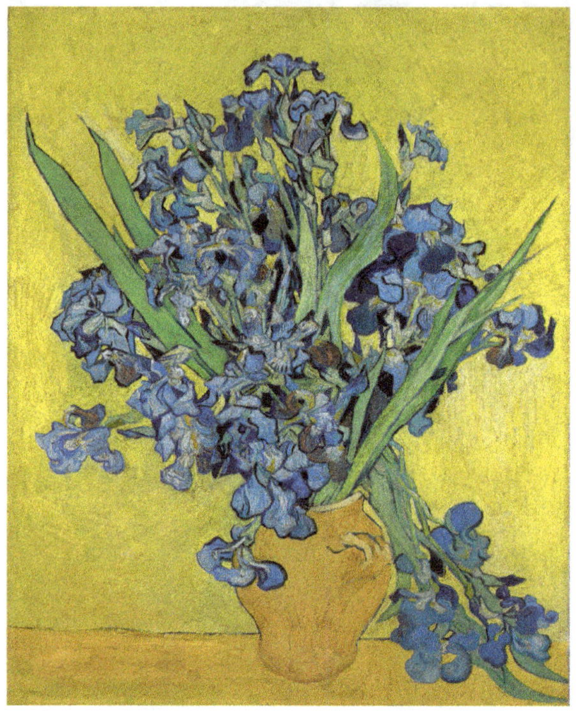

Vincent van Gogh, Irises, oil on canvas, May 1890

While in hospital in Saint-Rémy, Van Gogh painted many garden paintings where his use of color became almost autobiographic: in his own words, the combination of red, grey, green and thick black contours provoked anxiety.

The sky pictured in *Garden of the asylum* harbors a combination of bright colors in angled brushstrokes.

This has sometimes been explained as a result of the medication Van Gogh was taking, but remains open to interpretation.

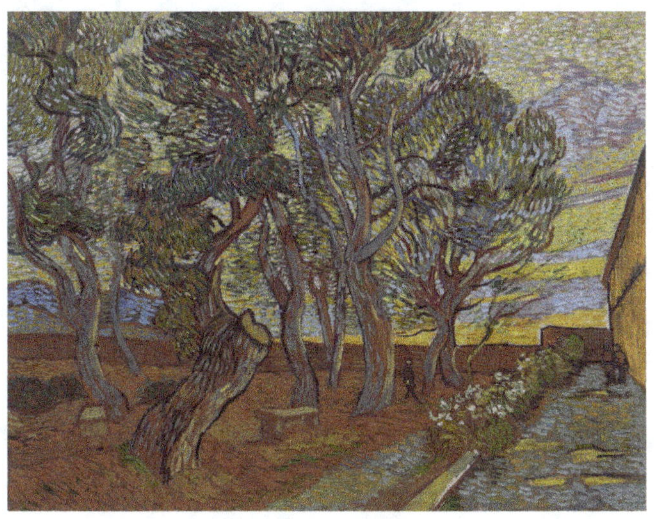

Vincent van Gogh, Garden of the Asylum, oil on canvas,
December 1889

A tender expression of brotherly love is incorporated into this painting of almond blossoms. Theo van Gogh had married and wrote to the painter in 1890, telling him that their newborn son had been named 'Vincent'.

Bursting with pride, the artist set to work on a painting of blossoms on branches. Almond blossoms are symbols of new life as they bloom very early in the southern regions of France.

The artist's nephew Vincent would later become the founder of the Van Gogh Foundation, managing the collection of the Van Gogh Museum.

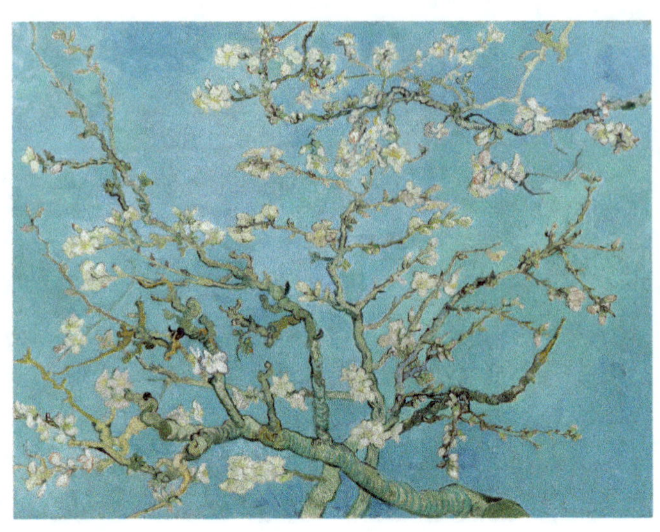

*Vincent van Gogh, Almond Blossom, oil on canvas, February
1890*

AUVERS-SUR-OISE (1890)

After leaving the hospital, Van Gogh went to live in Auvers-sur-Oise, a village close to Paris. It was here, in the last few months of his life, that he created a series of magnificent landscape paintings.

In *Wheatfield under Thunderclouds*, the clouds have become mere lumps of paint, and Van Gogh's style almost abstract.

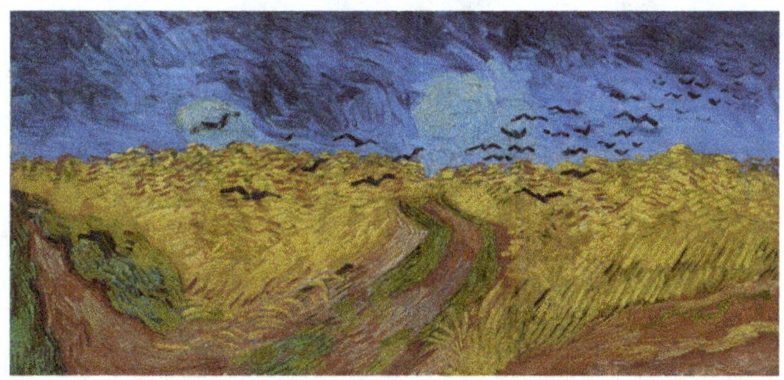

Vincent van Gogh, Wheatfield with Crows, oil on canvas, July 1890

This enigmatic landscape has long been regarded as Van Gogh's last painting. Though we now know that it is not his very last work, the sombre symbolism is difficult to overlook: the dark skies, the black crows, not to mention the ominous path leading nowhere.

The unfinished depiction of tree roots actually appears to be Van Gogh's last painting. Considering this painting was made only five years after *The Potato Eaters*, the development in such a short period of time is truly amazing.

Theo van Gogh's brother-in-law Andries Bonger alluded to the picture in a letter:

'The morning before his death, he had painted a sous-bois [forest scene], full of sun and life.'

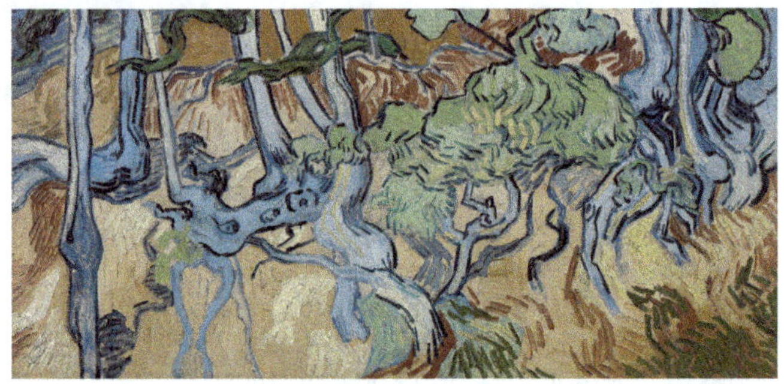

Vincent van Gogh, Tree Roots, oil on canvas, July 1890

OTHER ARTISTS IN THE COLLECTION

To provide visitors a better understanding of his full artistic development, the museum not only displays the artist's own work, but also works by influential contemporaries, as well as van Gogh's predecessors and followers. In the Rietveld building of the museum, you will find an extensive collection of paintings by artists related to Van Gogh in one way or another.

———

Characterised by bright colors and thick layers of paint, the works by the Dutch painter Kees van Dongen (1877 - 1968) were directly inspired by Van Gogh. They are in a style known as *Fauvisme,* or 'the style of wild animals'.

Fauvist artists aimed to work intuitively, with simple forms and bright colors. Van Dongen's favorite subject was the female body, which he called 'the most beautiful landscape there is'.

Portrayed here is Van Dongen's first wife, Guus Preitinger. Later in his career he became the portraitist of Parisian high society women like Brigitte Bardot.

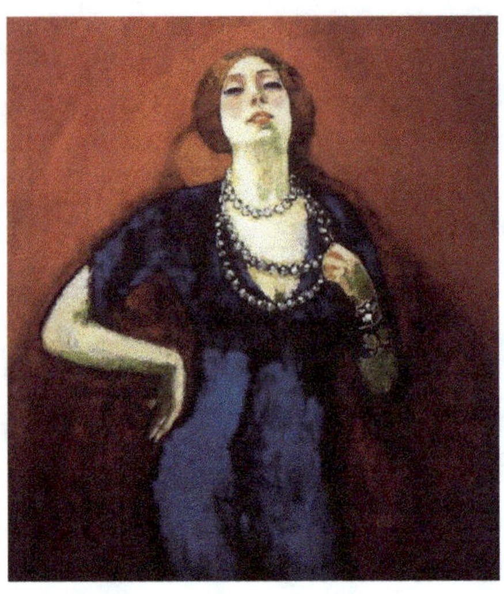

Kees van Dongen, Portrait of Guus Preitinger, the artist's wife, oil on canvas, 1911 © Kees van Dongen, De blauwe japon, 1911, c/o Pictoright Amsterdam 2017.

Kees van Dongen was popular as a portraitist of high society women. Rather sarcastically he observed that painting was the most beautiful of lies, and:

> "The essential thing is to elongate the women and especially to make them slim. After that it just remains to enlarge their jewels. They are ravished."

The self-portrait by Charles Laval (1862 - 1894) is the result of a deal the artist made with Van Gogh to exchange self-portraits.

Significantly, Laval did not place himself in the centre of the painting, but instead next to a window, offering us a view of the garden. Straight lines mark the window sills, yet the garden in the background appears more sketch-like.

Impressed with the painting, Van Gogh made a small drawing of it and included it in a letter to his brother Theo, describing it as 'very self-assured, very distinguished'.

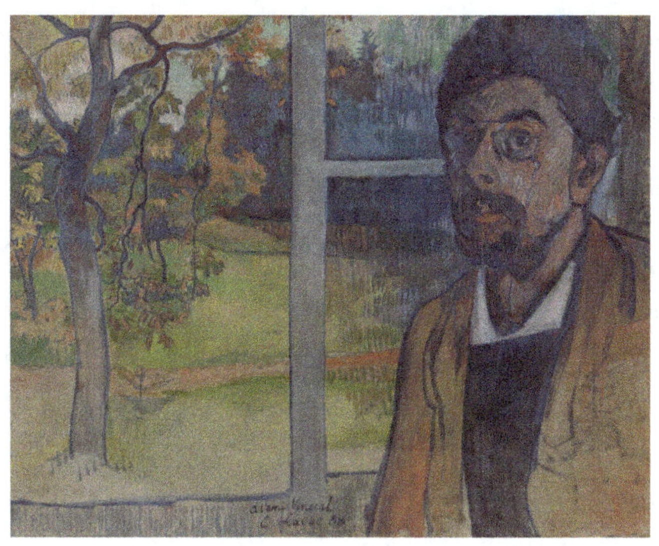

Charles Laval, Self-portrait, oil on canvas, 1888

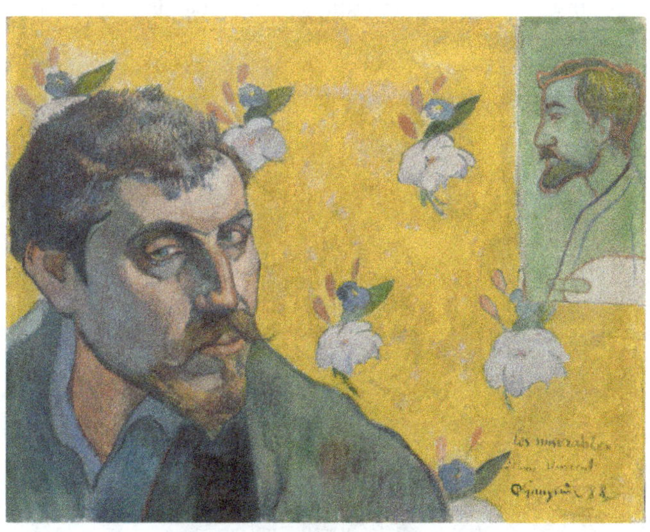

Paul Gauguin, Self-portrait with portrait of Émile Bernard (les misérables), oil on canvas, 1888

Paul Gauguin (1848 - 1903) portrayed himself in this painting as Jean Valjean, the protagonist in Victor Hugo's novel *'Les Misérables'*.

In Hugo's book, the hero is rejected by society but driven by inner convictions. As a painter in modern times, Gauguin considered himself to be in the same position, explaining his troubled expression, while the colors on the wall represent his purity as an artist.

In the background is a portrait of his close friend and colleague, Émile Bernard. Looking closely, you can also see Van Gogh in the bottom right corner, to whom this painting was dedicated.

1887 saw Paul Gauguin move to the Caribbean island of Martinique in an attempt to find inspiration in unspoiled surroundings. Holding a romantic view of life, he considered the natives of the island to be pure and noble savages with a direct connection to nature. This appealed to Gauguin as he sought spontaneity and authenticity.

Working in Martinique, he developed a new way of working with color. Yet for some art critics, the display of blue faces, green dogs, and purple trees was just 'evil'.

Gauguin loved the movements of the native women:

"Their gestures are quite extraordinary; their hands play an important role, in harmony with the swaying of their hips."

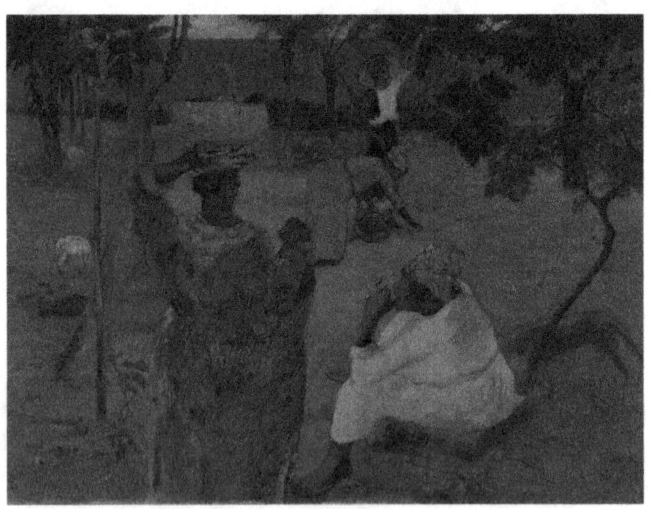

Paul Gauguin, The Mango trees, Martinique, oil on canvas, 1887

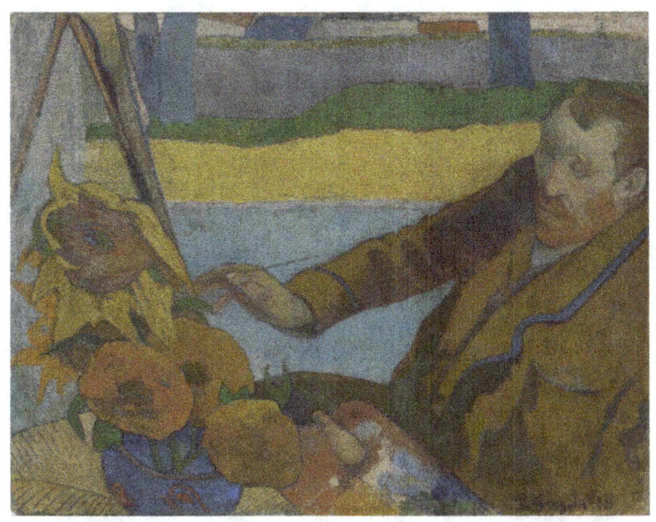

*Paul Gauguin, Vincent van Gogh painting Sunflowers, oil on
canvas, 1888*

In *Vincent van Gogh painting Sunflowers* Gauguin painted his friend
working on his famous sunflowers. Gauguin worked from the imagination,
since the flowers were not in season; the painting was executed in
December. This was one of the main areas of contention for the two artists:
Van Gogh preferred to work from life while Gauguin used his powers of
imagination.

When Van Gogh first saw the picture he was not pleased. He felt his friend
had depicted him as a madman, but softened his view later on. He wrote
to Theo:

> "My face has lit up after all a lot since, but it was indeed me, extremely
> tired and charged with electricity as I was then."

Flower still lifes became very popular in the 19th century. Without the
obligation to tell a story or capture a likeness, the painter was free to
experiment with shapes and colors.

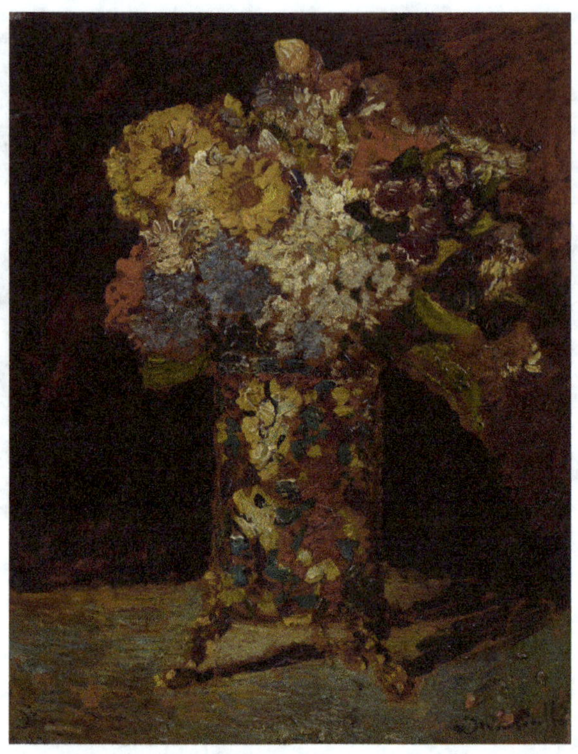

Adolphe Monticelli, Vase with flowers, oil on panel, circa 1875

When Theo van Gogh bought *Vase with flowers* by Adolphe Monticelli (1824 - 1886), his brother was ecstatic; he found the bright colors and the use of dots and stains instead of brushstrokes very inspiring. He asked his friends to buy him flowers, and then made a series of still lifes with the same composition.

In the 19th century, Jean François Millet (1814 - 1875) was at the forefront of a small but significant artistic revolution. Millet was the first to treat peasants as the subject in painting.

Before him, artists would regard them as picturesque elements in the background, no more important than animals, clouds and haystacks. Van Gogh admired Millet for his approach, and copied some of his works whilst being treated at the hospital in Saint-Rémy. During his stay in Saint-Rémy Van Gogh received a series of prints from Theo after paintings by Jean-François Millet. He 'translated' the black-and-white print into paintings in color. Below the Millet you will find one of these paintings by Van Gogh.

162

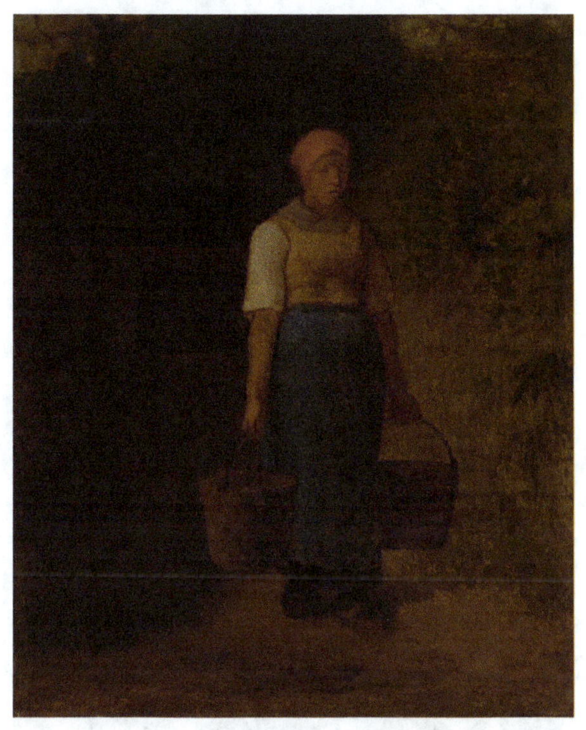

*Jean François Millet, Girl carrying water, oil on canvas, 1855 -
1860*

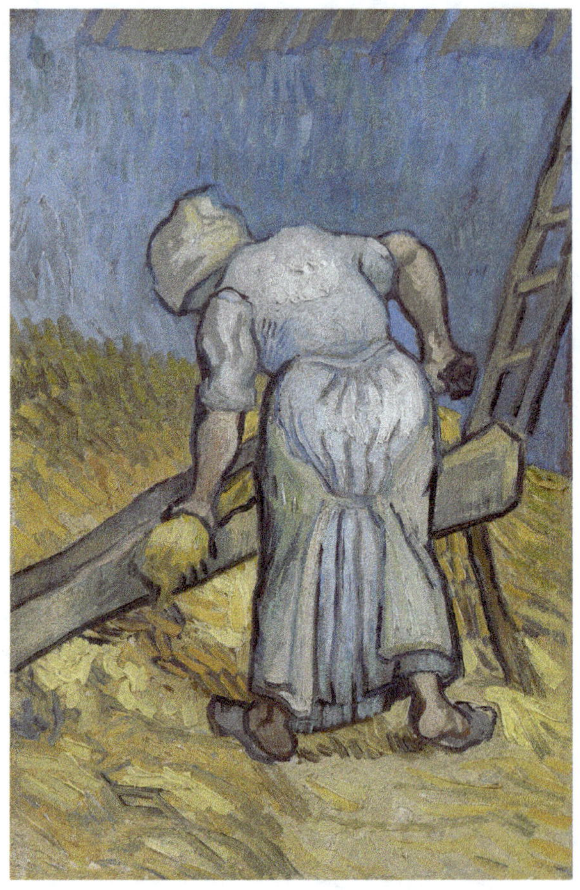

Vincent van Gogh, Peasant Woman bruising flax, oil on canvas,
1889

Due to his fondness for depictions of rural life, the works of the French painter Léon Augustin Lhermitte (1844 - 1925) interested Van Gogh greatly.

'I am too preoccupied by Lhermitte this evening to be able to talk of other things'.

The painting shows a group of farmers resting and repairing their tools. Though the scene appears informal, it is carefully staged - one can draw a circle to around the heads of the people portrayed, forming the centre of the composition. The horizon is high, allowing a gaze into the distance.

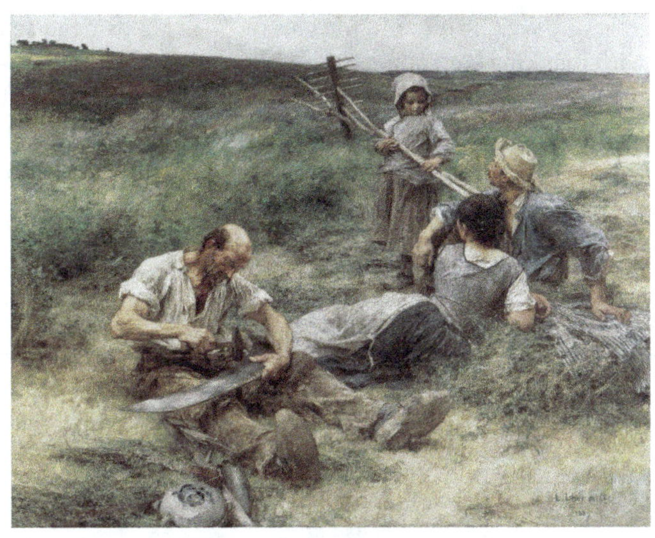

Léon-Augustin Lhermitte, Haymaking, oil on canvas, 1887

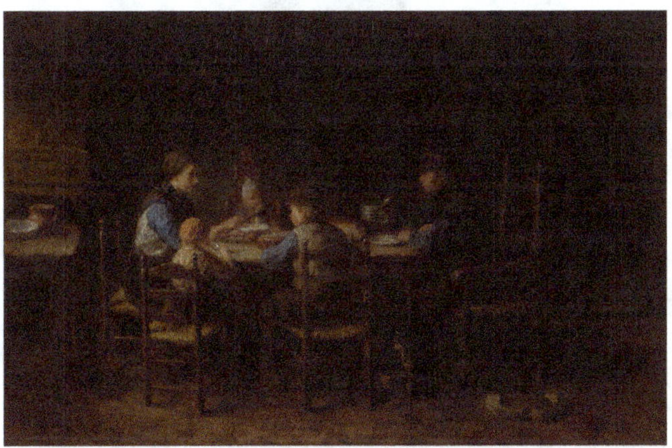

Jozef Israëls, Peasant Family at the table, oil on canvas, 1882

The painting of *Peasant Family at the table* by Jozef Israëls (1824 - 1911) is often shown with *The Potato Eaters* by Van Gogh.

Israëls was one of the most popular representatives of the Dutch so-called 'Hague School', whose painters focused on landscapes and the lives of farmers and fishermen.

This scene was a direct inspiration for Van Gogh, a realistic but sentimental portrayal with touching light effects and soft colors.

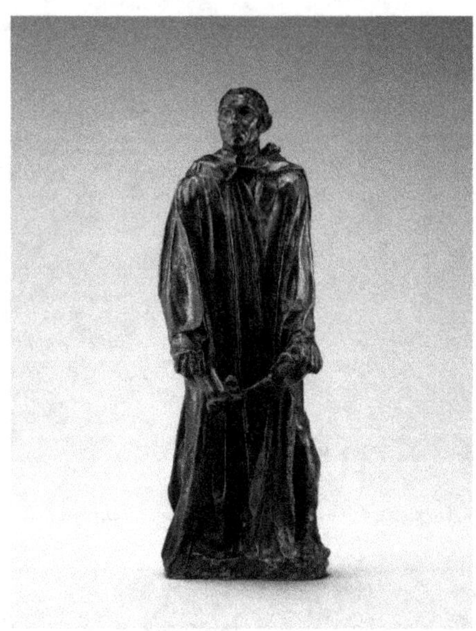

In 1884, the French sculptor, Auguste Rodin (1840 - 1917) received a commission to create a group of statues as a monument for the *Burghers of Calais*. These legendary figures attempted to save their city from pillaging by the English in 1346 by offering themselves as hostages and handing over the key to the city.

One of the statues of this group is in the Van Gogh Museum, and represents the burgher Jean d'Aire, showing his raw features and humble clothes. A grim expression disfigures his face: he is about to leave the city, in all likelihood facing death.

When exhibited, the monument was shown without a pedestal, allowing the viewer to feel the suffering and humiliation whilst walking through the group of statues.

Gustave Caillebotte, View seen through a balcony, oil on canvas,
1880

Like Van Gogh, the French painter Gustave Caillebotte (1848 - 1894) experimented with Japanese elements. In this painting, the wrought-iron balcony dominates the foreground while Avenue Hausman is placed to the back, with people and horses shown merely as shadowy figures. Rather than the view on the Boulevard, the cast-iron curly pattern of the balcony is the actual subject of this modern painting.

The landscape illustrated below is painted by Camille Pissarro (1831 - 1903) who was a major influence on Van Gogh. Using dots, stripes and bright colors, it shows the haymaking in August. It is easy to draw comparisons when looking at Van Gogh's *Square St. Pierre*, painted in Paris (see Paris section). The other artist was so important to Van Gogh that he was nicknamed 'Father Pissarro'.

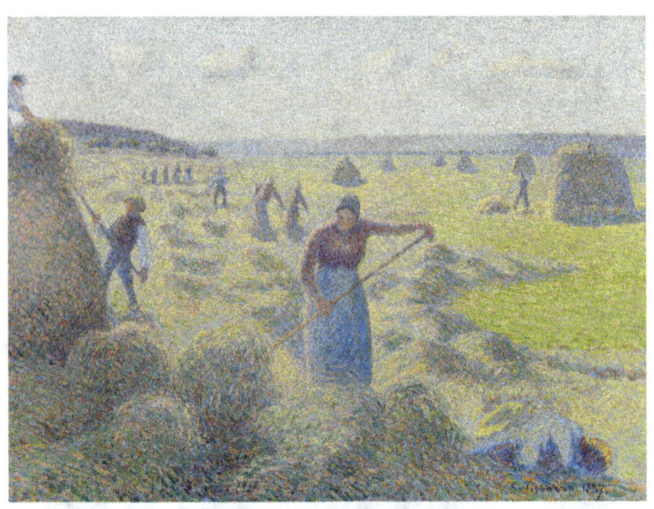

Camille Pissarro, *Haymaking, Éragny, oil on canvas, 1887*

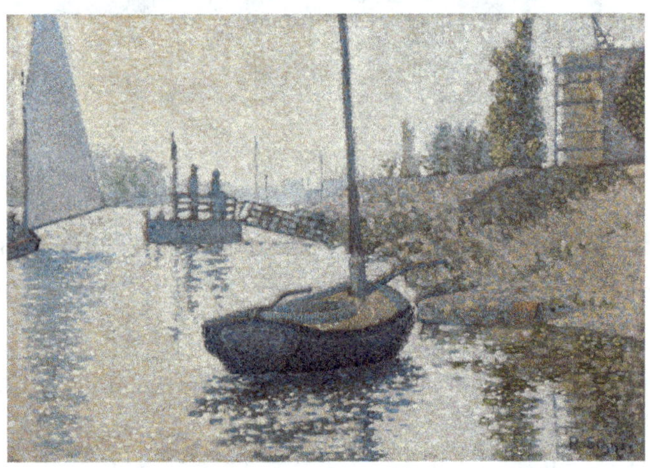

The *"Ponton de la Félicité" at Asnières (Opus no. 143) Paul
Signac, 1886*

The *"Ponton de la Félicité" at Asnières (Opus no. 143)* is the first pointillist painting by Signac in the Van Gogh Museum, filling an important gap in its collection. Paul Signac painted this in 1886 on the banks of the Seine near Asnières.

Van Gogh and Signac met in Paris in 1887. Both artists often went to Asnières to paint on the banks of the river Seine. Van Gogh admired by Signac's free application of the pointillist technique, and his use of bright, complementary colors. Although Van Gogh himself only made a couple of works using a strictly pointillist style, this manner of painting became the basis of his characteristic style, which features expressive dashes and short lines of pure color placed next to one another.

With regard to Signac's influence on the development of Van Gogh's work, artist friend Emile Bernard said:

> "He [Van Gogh] was already in the process of 'changing his palette' and, acting on Signac's advice, was experimenting with a free form of divisionism."

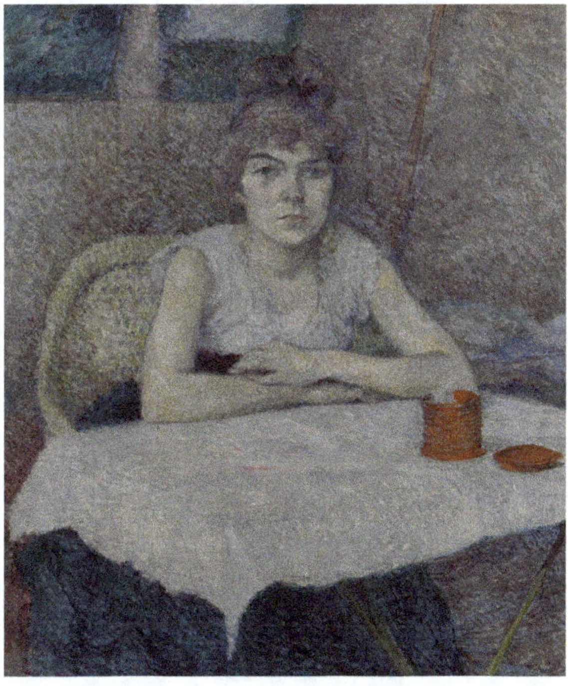

Henri de Toulouse-Lautrec, Young woman at a table, 'poudre de riz', oil on canvas, 1887

This woman has often been referred to as Suzanne Valadon, the mistress of Henri de Toulouse-Lautrec (1864 - 1901), a close friend of Van Gogh. It is not sure that it is her actually. The two artists met at the Atelier Cormon in Paris where both studied for a while.

The painting is called *Poudre de riz*, or 'rice powder', named after the red jar on the table containing make-up. Rice was used to achieve a pale complexion, a sign of beauty. When you are in the museum you will see that the paint surface is rather matt. Toulouse Lautrec used a blotting paper to remove the glossy oil from the paint, which was then diluted with turpentine. The technique was popular among modern painters.

On Van Gogh's recommendation Theo van Gogh bought *Poudre de riz* for their collection. Since he did not earn a penny with his own work, Van Gogh thought it was a good investment that they (i.e. Theo) would acquire works of art by their contemporaries and thus create their own collection of modern art. In this process Van Gogh acted at the advisor. All of these pictures can nowadays be seen at the Van Gogh museum.

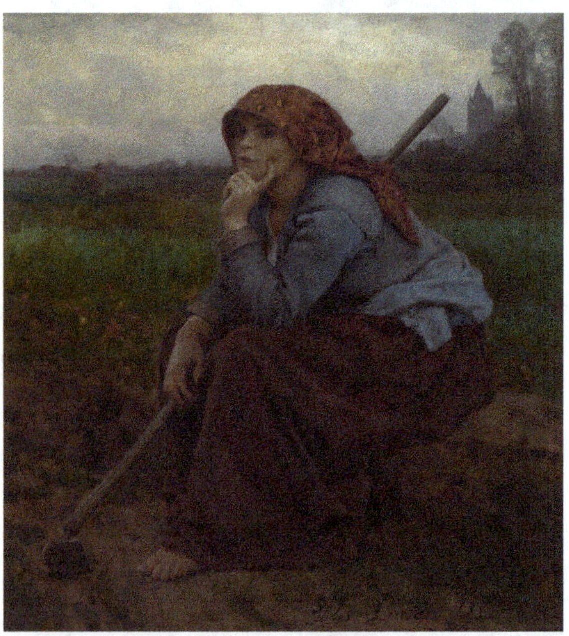

Jules Breton, Young peasant girl with a hoe, oil on canvas on panel, 1882

Van Gogh admired Millet and also the French painter and poet, Jules Breton (1827 - 1905), both painters of rural scenes. Even though Breton was a realist painter, this image betrays a hint of sentimentalism. The peasant girl stares out of the picture; her eyes are pensive and tones muted. Van Gogh was no enemy of the sentimental, stating that 'one must have imaginative power and sentiment while painting'. Like Van Gogh, Breton followed in the footsteps of painters with an interest in country life and realism, such as Jean-François Millet.

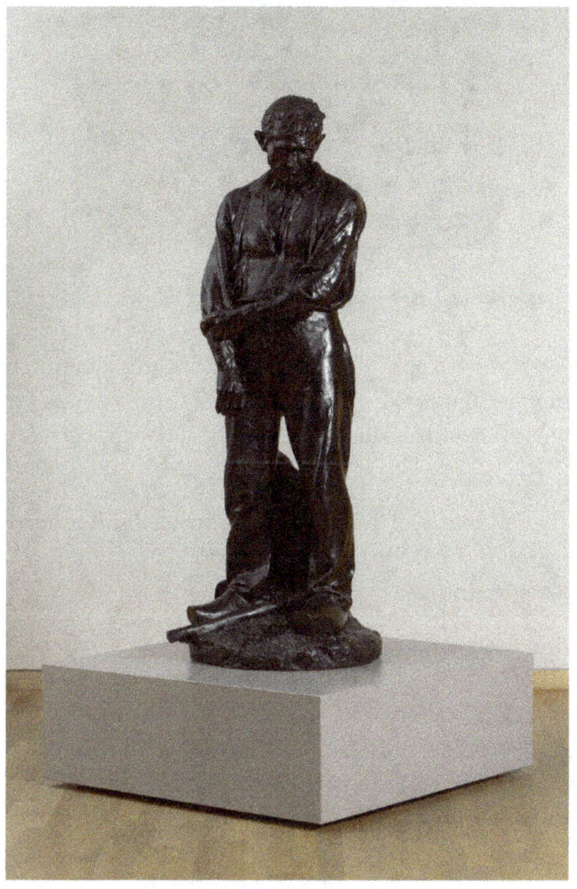

Aimé Jules Dalou, Tall peasant, bronze, 1898 - 99 (design circa 1899, cast 1902 - 1905)

This statue of a farmer rolling up his sleeves would have been very much to Van Gogh's taste. Like in *The Potato Eaters*, the subject is the hard-working common man, portrayed with dignity. The sculptor Aimé Jules Dalou (1838 - 1901) was a working-class hero. Born a laborer's son, he knew the hardships of ordinary people only too well. In his work, he gave these people a face.

Like Rodin's statue of Jean d'Aire, the statue of the tall peasant was part of a group of sculptures glorifying labor.

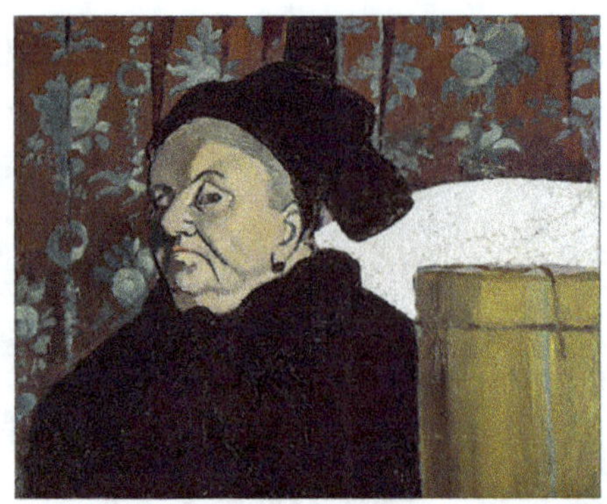

Émile Bernard, Portrait of his Grandmother, oil on canvas, 1887

While Van Gogh was supported, personally and financially, by his brother Theo, the French painter Émile Bernard (1868 - 1941) relied on his grandmother, Mrs. Bodin-Lallement, a lady who appears regularly in his paintings.

Like many other painters of his day, Bernard was influenced by Japanese art, as can be seen in the large planes of color, clear contours and magnified details in the foreground.

In his days as an assistant minister in England, Van Gogh often mentioned the paintings by the English artist George Henry Boughton (1833 - 1904) in his sermons. Van Gogh was especially enthusiastic about the work showing pilgrims setting out for Canterbury. He would often tell his congregation, 'life is a voyage towards God', and in this painting one can see pilgrims having their flasks filled with water as they are on their way to Canterbury.

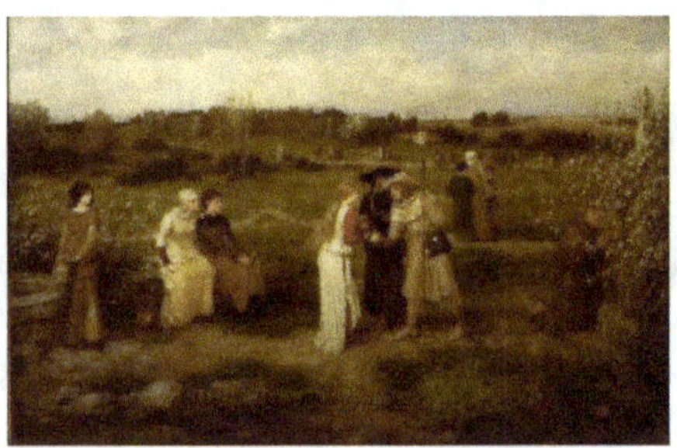

George Henry Boughton, Godspeed! Pilgrims setting out for Canterbury, oil on canvas, 1874

PRACTICAL INFORMATION

Time-slotted admission tickets regulate visitor distribution. The peaks and lows of visitor flows are less pronounced than they used to be, and visitors are distributed more evenly throughout the entire day. One in four visitors purchases a ticket online in advance.

Extended opening hours on Fridays (and in the summer months also on Saturdays) allow the museum to deal with the busy summer period. Often people are not aware of the fact that the museum is open on Friday until 10 pm, so that also may be a good time to visit.

If you wish to visit during the day, is advisable to go there between 9 am and 11 am, or after 3 pm.

Try to avoid the busiest times which are between 11 am and 3 pm.

Please note: last admission is 30 minutes before closing time.

You can order entrance tickets online for direct access at your preferred time and date. Tickets are available four months in advance.

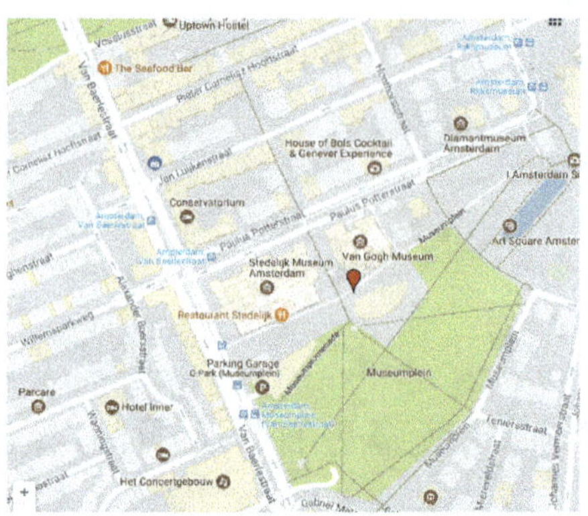

Map of Museumplein Amsterdam

HERMITAGE AMSTERDAM

HIGHLIGHTS FROM THE HERMITAGE
MUSEUM ST PETERSBURG

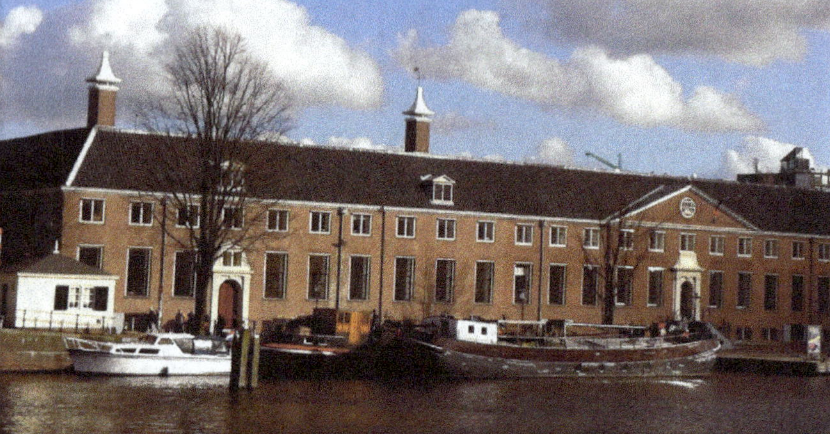

MARKO KASSENAAR

Highlights from the Hermitage Museum St Petersburg

HERMITAGE AMSTERDAM

INTRODUCTION

Hermitage Amsterdam is the newest of the top five museums in Amsterdam. The museum functions as a branch of the State Hermitage Museum in St Petersburg, Russia but is an independent legal entity.

Art from the legendary Russian collection is displayed to the public in temporary exhibitions. Beautifully located alongside the River Amstel, Hermitage Amsterdam has been popular with tourists and locals alike since it opened its doors in June 2009.

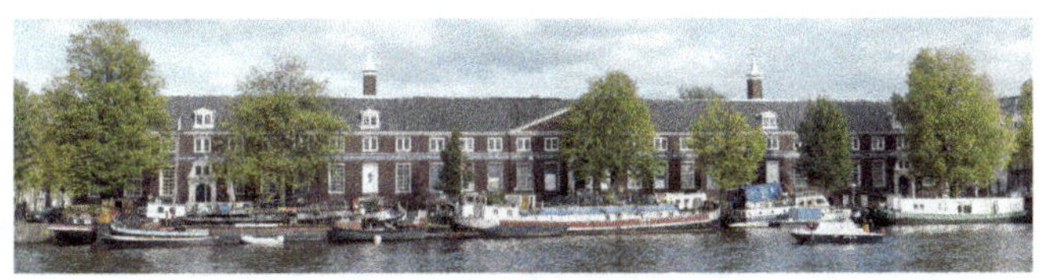

Hermitage Amsterdam © Wikimedia Commons

The museum has two wings for exhibitions, a concert hall, a library and a café-style restaurant that stays open after the museum closes in the evening. The spacious inner courtyard is used for open air opera performances in summer.

Hermitage Amsterdam generally has no collection of its own, and instead relies on rotating displays. Every year, new exhibitions are organized consisting of top pieces from the museum in St Petersburg. You will find an exhibition program at the end of this short guide.

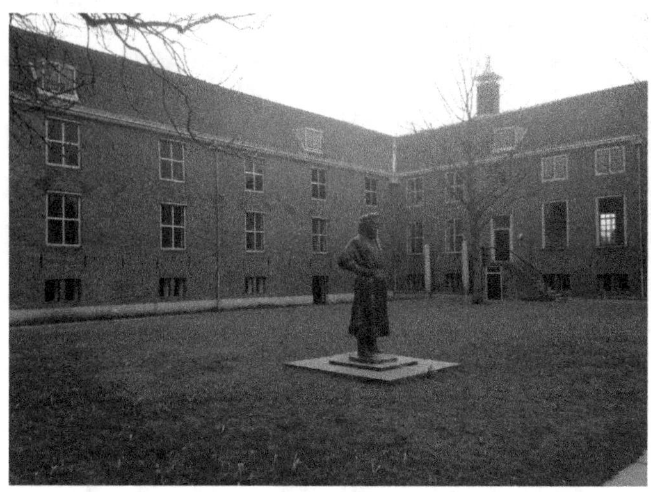

Statue of Rembrandt in the courtyard of the Hermitage
Amsterdam, Picture by the Publisher

PORTRAIT GALLERY OF THE
GOLDEN AGE

The Hermitage Amsterdam has on permanent display over thirty very large 17th-century group portraits that can be regarded as the artistic siblings of Rembrandt's *Nightwatch*.

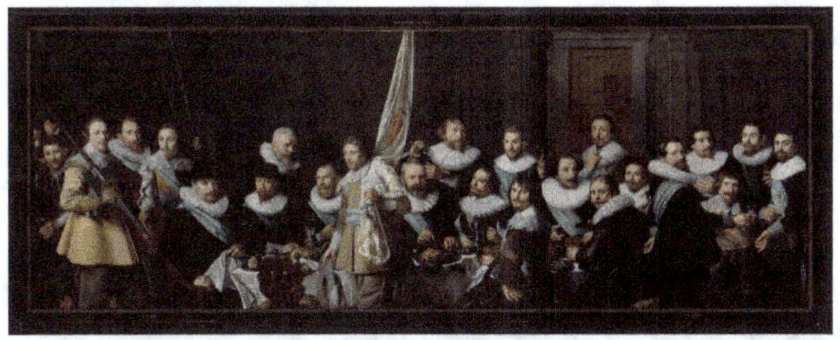

*Nicolaes Eliasz Pickenoy (1591-1653), Banquet of the civic
guards from the company of captain Jacob Backer and lieutenant
Jacob Rogh, 1632. 198 x 531 cm. Collection Amsterdam
Museum; inv.nr. SA 7313.*

Due to their enormous proportions the portraits are rarely on view, let alone shown together in a single exhibition. The works come from the collections of the Amsterdam Museum as well as the Rijksmuseum in Amsterdam.

In these portraits you can see merchants, civic guards, regents, regentesses and archers from various backgrounds and religions. They reflect the spirit of collective citizenship that characterized the Netherlands in the 17th century.

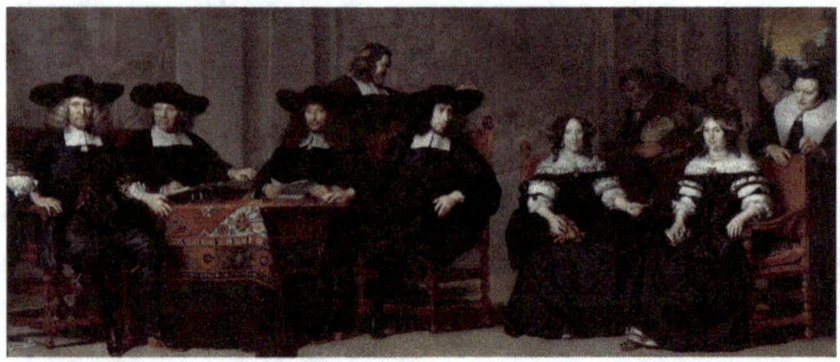

Adriaen Backer (1630-1684), The governors and governesses of
the old men- and women's house, 1676. 197 x 457 cm. Collection
Amsterdam Museum; inv nr. SA 991

The Republic of the Seven United Netherlands was ruled by the bourgeoisie, unlike the rest of Europe where power was concentrated in the hands of a monarch or church official. This exhibition allows visitors to come face to face with the men and women that made the Netherlands into a world-leading and prosperous state.

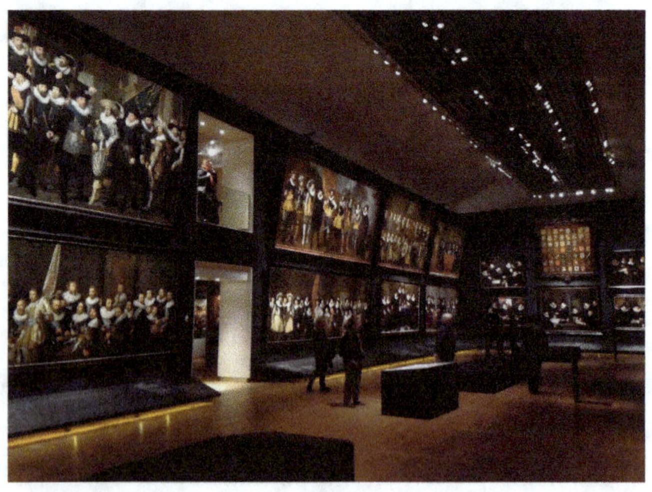

Portrait Gallery of the Golden Age, Picture by the Publisher

The *Nightwatch* has familiarized audiences with large-scale portraits of the members of the city's civic guard. Other members of upper-class society that often had their portraits painted include the men and women in charge of the administration of care and disciplinary institutions. Portrayed seated at large tables, occupied by business, these regents and regentesses wanted to record their good governance and charitable work. Craft guilds could also afford to commission portraits, especially the Amsterdam Guild of Surgeons, whose members can be spotted in the paintings depicting anatomy lessons.

The top floor of the museum addresses the society reflected in the Dutch group portraits of the Golden Age through historical images as well as audiovisual presentations. Themes like egalitarianism, tolerance and liberty are explored from the 17th century until the present, connecting the outlook of the contemporary nation with that of its 400-year-old ancestor.

If you want to see how this unique exhibition came together please view this YouTube film:

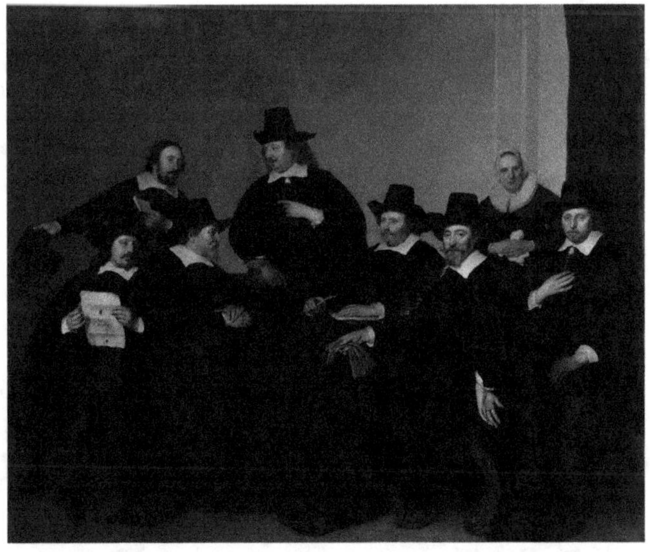

Jacob Backer (1608/09-1651), The governors of the Nieuwezijds Huiszittenhuis in Amsterdam, ca 1650, 272 x 312 cm, Collection Rijksmuseum, inv nr. SK-C-442

HISTORY OF THE MUSEUM

At the end of the 20th century, plans were made to open an affiliation of the State Hermitage Museum in St Petersburg. To reach a wider audience, this secondary location had to be found outside Russia.

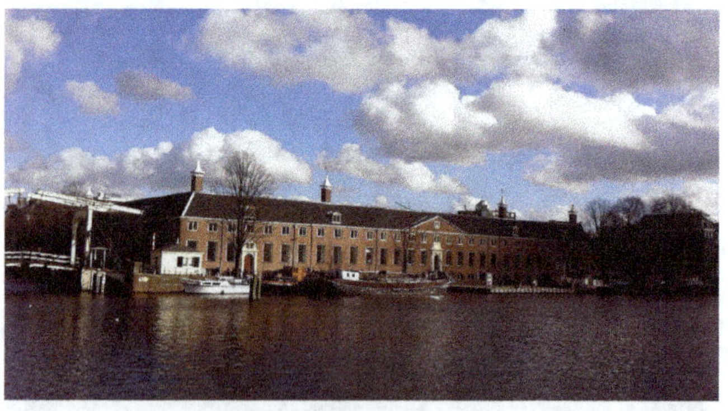

Hermitage Amsterdam, Picture by the Publisher

The incentive for this undertaking was the size of the collection - the Hermitage houses more than 3 million objects, most of them stored in warehouses. Amsterdam was chosen for making these hidden treasures available to the public.

There is a historic connection between this city and St Petersburg. Czar Peter the Great visited the Netherlands in 1697, wanting to learn about the techniques of reclaiming land and building cities in marshlands, topics on which the Dutch were experts. Peter the Great then founded his own city inspired by Amsterdam, St Petersburg, with characteristic canals, bridges and warehouses. Dutch engineers travelled to Russia to help the Czar oversee the building process.

In the 19th century, the Netherlands and Russia further strengthened their connection through the marriage of the Dutch King Willem II and Anna Paulowna, daughter of the Russian Czar. Today, the economic and cultural ties between the two countries remain strong.

In the 1990s, the New Church (Dutch: 'Nieuwe Kerk') on Dam Square organised several exhibitions with works from the Hermitage, St Petersburg. This collaboration, in combination with the historic ties, made Amsterdam the obvious choice for the new Hermitage franchise. In 2009, the museum was opened by Queen Beatrix of the Netherlands and President Dmitri Medvedev of Russia. Since its opening, the museum has played host to a million visitors each year.

The museum overlooks the Amstel, the waterway that gave Amsterdam its name. Symbolically, the restaurant in the Hermitage Amsterdam is named 'Neva', after the river in St Petersburg.

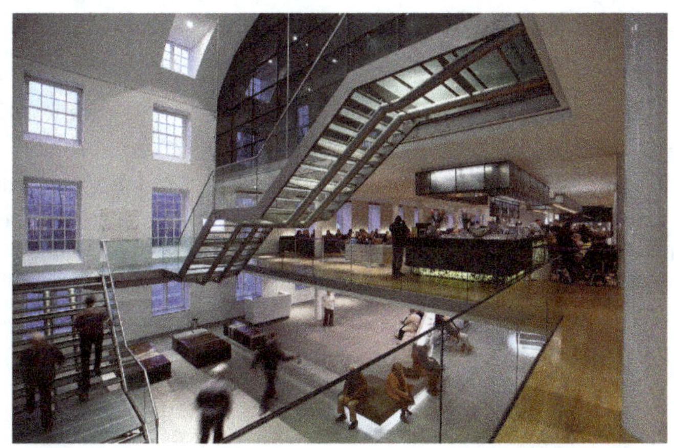

Interior view of Hermitage Amsterdam © Photography Jørgen Koopmanschap

THE BUILDING

The Hermitage Amsterdam is situated in a building called 'Amstelhof', a former nursing home providing shelter for 400 elderly women.

In order to be eligible to live there, the women had to be over 50 years old, a member of the Church for a minimum of ten years and a resident of Amsterdam for at least fifteen years. It remained a nursing home until 2004.

The building became a museum in 2009 after extensive renovation. The bedrooms have become exhibition rooms and the great halls form the starting points of each exhibition. The church is used for concerts and in summer there are festivities in the garden, such as festivals and opera performances.

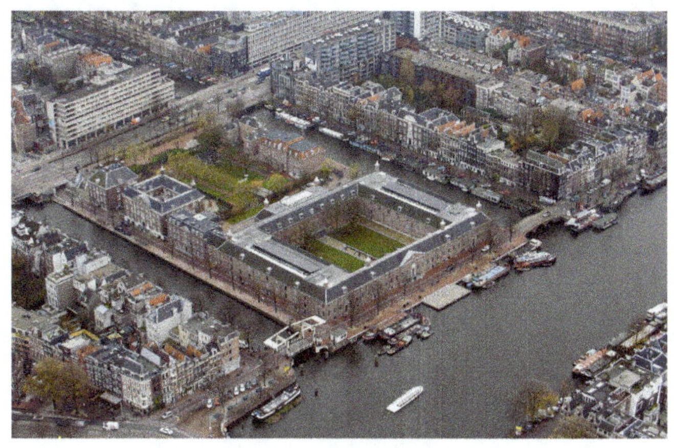

Birdseye view Hermitage © Photo by Wooning Aviation

The interior of the museum is light and open-plan. Every year, the interior is adjusted to the new masterpieces arriving from the Hermitage, St Petersburg.

EXHIBITION PROGRAM

16 June 2018 - 13 January 2019: **Classic Beauties**

The exhibition *Classic Beauties* will offer a delightful journey through European Neoclassicism, including the unrivelled Canova collection with *The Three Graces*.

Winter 2018/19 - Summer 2019: **Catherine the Great**

Spring 2018 - Winter 2018/19: **European Neoclassicism**

Summer 2019 - Winter 2019/20: **Greek and Scythian Gold**

The exhibition program is subject to change, so if you want to see the most up-to-date program, click here to go to the Hermitage Amsterdam website.

LOCATION AND TICKETS

For up-to-date information on opening hours and ticket prices, please visit the website of the Hermitage Amsterdam.

Advance tickets can be bought through the Hermitage Amsterdam website, and via: +31 (0)20 530 87 55.

The museum is open daily from 10 am to 5 pm. Waiting times can vary.

There is limited parking in the immediate surroundings of the museum. Nearest parking facilities: Muziektheater.

The museum can be reached by public transport. From Amsterdam Central Station, take tram 9, and get off at Waterlooplein. Other options are metro 51, 53 or 54, stop Waterlooplein, exit Nieuwe Herengracht.

Audio tours are available in various languages in the entrance hall of the museum.

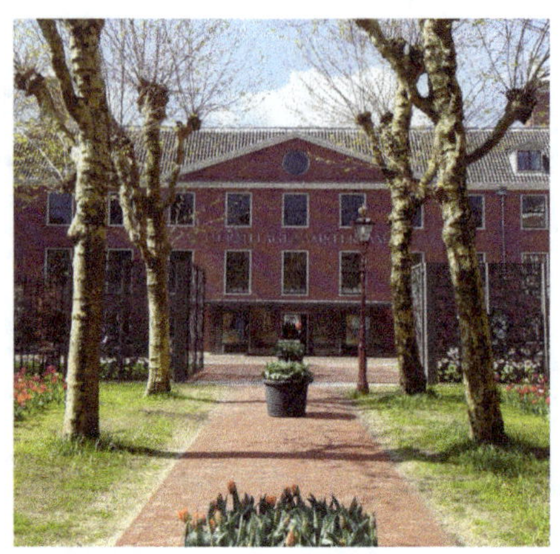

Hermitage Amsterdam © Photo by Janiek Dam

OTHER MUSEUMS NEAR HERMITAGE AMSTERDAM

The Hermitage Amsterdam is located in the center of Amsterdam, within a 10-minute walk of three other top museums.

The Rembrandt House museum is located in the house where the famous painter lived from 1639 to 1658. It has been redecorated in 17th-century style, and includes the artist's workshop. A selection of his etchings is displayed on one of the top floors. The museumshop is well worth a visit. Address: Jodenbreestraat 4

The Jewish Historical Museum focuses on Jewish history and culture. It is located at the heart of the former Jewish Quarter of Amsterdam. Address: Nieuwe Amstelstraat 1.

The Resistance Museum takes the visitor back to the days when Holland was occupied by Germany during World War II. Address: Plantage Kerklaan 61A.

FURTHER READING SUGGESTIONS

We invite you to have a look at the following books in the series *Secrets of Van Gogh,* all of which are available as eBook and paperback.

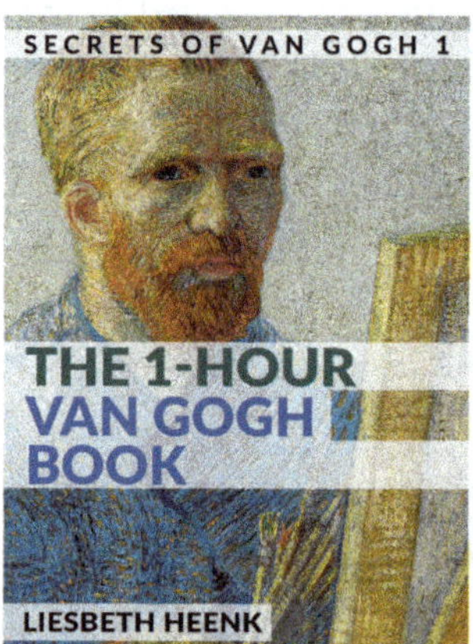

1. *The 1-Hour Van Gogh Book. Complete Van Gogh Biography for Beginners* is a brief introduction to Van Gogh's fascinating life and work.

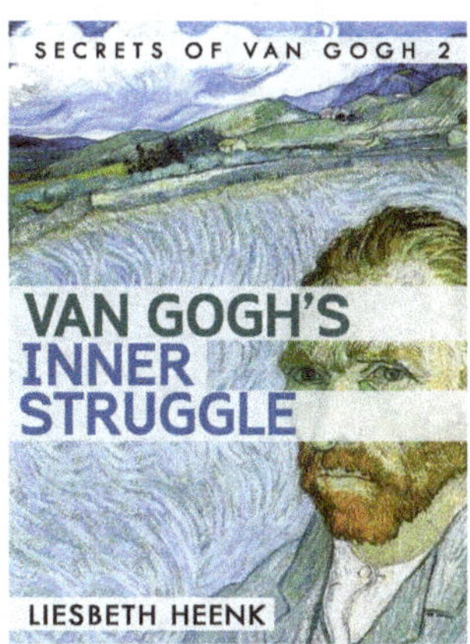

2. *Van Gogh's Inner Struggle: Life, Work and Mental Illness* concentrates on the artist's life, approach to work and his mental illness.

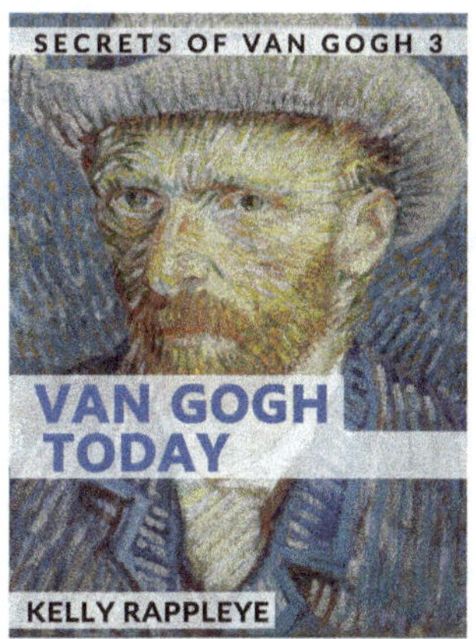

3. *Van Gogh Today - Short Stories* contains eight short stories of lives that were touched in some way or another by the artist. They are a reflection of the power of his story, and why Van Gogh remains a timeless inspiration to us all.

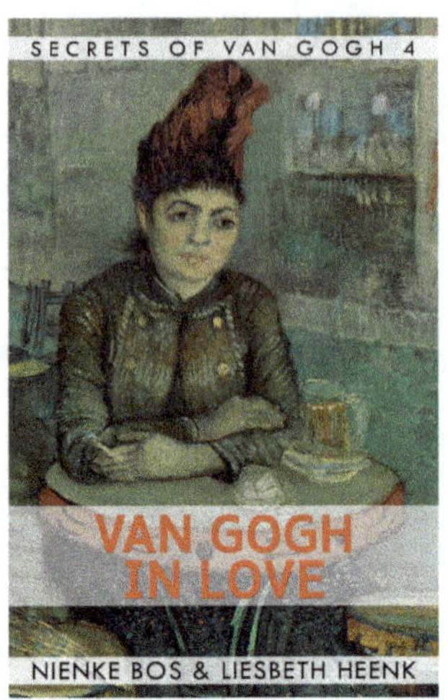

4. *Van Gogh in Love - a (not so!) romantic Van Gogh Biography* tells the story of the artist's longing for love and a family, exploring the lesser-known area of the artist's romantic life. As can perhaps be expected from an artist like Vincent van Gogh, his choice of women was unconventional. He favored more mature companions, and pursued relationships with women that were considered unsuitable.

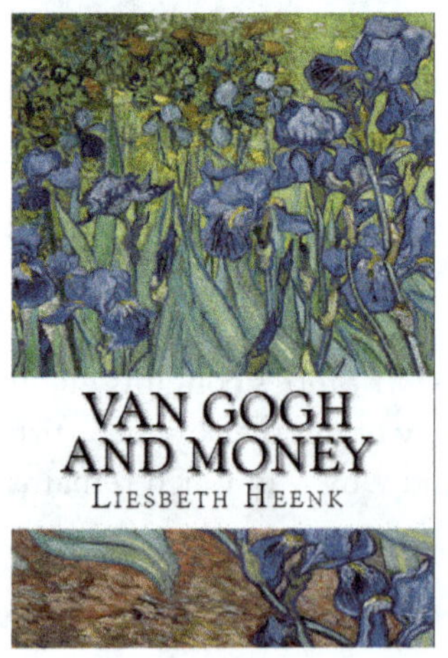

5. *Van Gogh and Money – The Myth of the Poor Artist* focuses on Van Gogh's financial situation, a subject never explored before. Known as the

ultimate embodiment of the notion of the "poor artist", Van Gogh was largely unable to sell his work. His letters tell of an eternal lack of money, and the difficulties this created. But how poor was Van Gogh actually?

———

If you want to know more about Rembrandt's etchings, we invite you to have a look at the following book which is available as eBook and paperback.

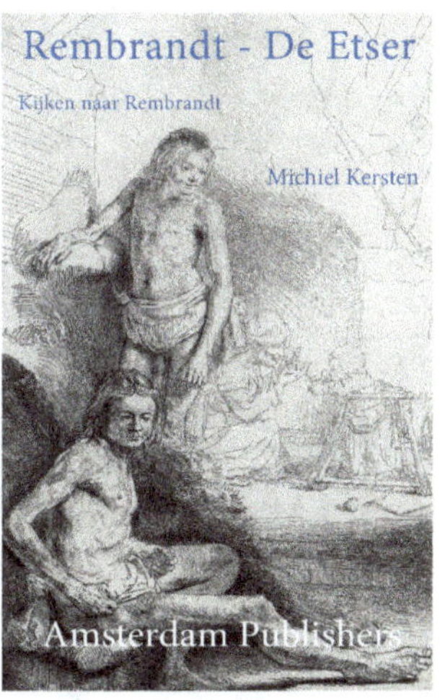

Rembrandt Etchings, Looking at Rembrandt's Prints

In his day, Rembrandt was better known as an etcher than as a painter. Looking at Rembrandt's prints requires a little time and patience from the viewer, but the rewards are enormous. Rembrandt moved expertly between genres, demonstrating his ingenuity, insight into human emotion and mastery of the etching medium in every image. The compositions are beautifully balanced despite a wealth of narrative detail. Every line has a purpose - nothing is accidental or left to chance.

This Rembrandt Etchings book will guide you on your visual journey of discovery, and allow you to see why Rembrandt was the greatest of all seventeenth century printmakers. By reading it you will learn a great deal about the technical aspect of printmaking, Rembrandt's choice of papers, his expertise in marketing his etchings, and prints are discussed per genre. The book contains high-quality illustrations.

The book has been written by an expert in the field of Dutch seventeenth century art, Michiel Kersten. He refrains from using art historical jargon, so that everyone interested in getting to know Rembrandt will be able to enjoy this book.

COLOPHON

Things to do in Amsterdam: Museums consists of 4 different Amsterdam Museum Guides.

Volume 1: *Rijksmuseum Amsterdam. Highlights of the Collection*

Authors: Marko Kassenaar & Liesbeth Heenk

Editor: Malin Lönnberg

ISBN 13: 9789492371348 (ebook)

ISBN 13: 9789492371331 (paperback)

Illustrations of art works are courtesy and copyright of the Rijksmuseum in Amsterdam. Illustration of the cover: copyright of Wikipedia – Creative Commons.

Volume 2: *Anne Frank House Amsterdam. Anne's Secret Annex turned into Museum*

Authors: Marko Kassenaar & Liesbeth Heenk

ISBN 13: 9789492371652 (ebook)

ISBN 13: 9781496053534 (paperback)

Volume 3: *Van Gogh Museum Amsterdam. Highlights of the Collection*

Authors: Marko Kassenaar & Liesbeth Heenk

Publisher: Amsterdam Publishers, The Netherlands

ISBN 13 : 9789492371379 (paperback)

ISBN 13 : 9789492371386 (ebook)

Volume 4: *Hermitage Amsterdam. Highlights from the Hermitage Museum St Petersburg*

Authors: Marko Kassenaar & Liesbeth Heenk

Publisher: Amsterdam Publishers, The Netherlands

ISBN 13: 9789492371669 (ebook)